Lecture Notes in Computer Science 13430

Founding Editors

Gerhard Goos

Juris Hartmanis

Editorial Board Members

The series Lecture Notes in Computer Science (LNCS), including its subseries Lecture Notes in Artificial Intelligence (LNAI) and Lecture Notes in Bioinformatics (LNBI), has established itself as a medium for the publication of new developments in computer science and information technology research, teaching, and education.

LNCS enjoys close cooperation with the computer science R & D community, the series counts many renowned academics among its volume editors and paper authors, and collaborates with prestigious societies. Its mission is to serve this international community by providing an invaluable service, mainly focused on the publication of conference and workshop proceedings and postproceedings. LNCS commenced publication in 1973.

José Ángel Bañares · Jörn Altmann ·
Orna Agmon Ben-Yehuda · Karim Djemame ·
Vlado Stankovski · Bruno Tuffin
Editors

Economics of Grids, Clouds, Systems, and Services

19th International Conference, GECON 2022
Izola, Slovenia, September 13–15, 2022
Proceedings

Editors
José Ángel Bañares (iD)
University of Zaragoza
Zaragoza, Spain

Orna Agmon Ben-Yehuda (iD)
University of Haifa
Haifa, Israel

Vlado Stankovski (iD)
University of Ljubljana
Ljubljana, Slovenia

Jörn Altmann (iD)
Seoul National University
Seoul, Korea (Republic of)

Karim Djemame (iD)
University of Leeds
Leeds, UK

Bruno Tuffin (iD)
Inria Rennes - Bretagne Atlantique
Rennes, France

ISSN 0302-9743   ISSN 1611-3349 (electronic)
Lecture Notes in Computer Science
ISBN 978-3-031-29314-6   ISBN 978-3-031-29315-3 (eBook)
https://doi.org/10.1007/978-3-031-29315-3

Preface

This volume constitutes the proceedings of the 19th International Conference on the Economics of Grids, Clouds, Systems, and Services (GECON 2022). This series of conferences serves as a meeting place, to bring together distributed systems expertise (e.g., in resource allocation, quality of service management, and energy consumption) with economics expertise (focusing on both micro- and macro-economic modelling and analysis) to create effective solutions in this space. GECON continues to focus on the marriage of these two types of expertise, reinforced by the increasing intertwinement of economy and technology. The adoption of a multidisciplinary approach allows the GECON community of scientists and practitioners to maintain and build strong links between ICT technical expertise and economic expertise.

GECON 2022 was held during September 13–15, 2022, organized by the Faculty of Computer and Information Science of the University of Ljubljana, Slovenia. This year's edition of the GECON conference was celebrated in a hybrid format combining in-situ with online presentations and participants. The in-situ conference was held in the exceptionally touristic city of Izola, located in southwestern Slovenia. The conference took place at the San Simon Resort, offering both high-level conference facilities and wonderful views of the Adriatic coast.

This year, we received 22 submissions in response to our call for papers. Each paper was single-blind peer-reviewed by at least four members of the international Program Committee. Based on significance, novelty, and scientific quality, we selected 4 full papers (18% acceptance rate), which are included in this volume. Additionally, 6 work-in-progress papers, 4 new ideas papers, and two invited papers were integrated into the volume.

This volume has been structured following the sessions that comprised the conference program:

- Special GECON topics
- Business Models, Service Discovery
- Serverless Computing, IoT, Edge, Resource Management
- New Idea Papers

The two invited articles (special GECON topics) of this year's GECON are based on one keynote and one tutorial:

The keynote speaker on the first day was Ian J. Taylor, CTO of SIMBA Chain. Ian's keynote "The Curation, Interfacing and Analysis Lifecycle of Blockchain Applications" focused on the lifecycle of Web3 applications, describing ways in which next-generation decentralised applications can be orchestrated, curated, executed, and analysed. The content of this keynote is captured in the first invited paper.

The keynote speaker on the second day was Elisabetta Di Nitto, professor at Politecnico di Milano. Her keynote "Infrastructure as Code: State of the Art and Practice, Challenges and Possible Solutions with Model-Driven Engineering" presented the deployment of cloud applications and the correct management of their lifecycle as a critical and complex task. As part of the DevOps tactics, Infrastructure-as-Code (IaC) provides the ability to create, configure, and manage complex infrastructures by means of executable code. Writing IaC, however, is not an easy task, since it requires blending different infrastructure programming languages and abstractions, each specialised on a particular aspect of infrastructure creation, configuration, and management. Moreover, the more software system architectures become large and complex (think, for instance, of data-intensive or microservice-based architectures), the more dire the need for IaC becomes. In this talk, Elisabetta provided an overview of the state of the art and practice in IaC, and of the main challenges in this area. Furthermore, she showed how model-driven approaches can help to address some of these challenges.

On the third day, the keynote speaker Ittay Eyal, assistant professor in the faculty of Electrical Engineering at Technion, presented "Blockchain Incentive-Based Security". The security of blockchain protocols critically relies on incentive compatibility. This talk reviewed the basic principles of game-theoretical analysis of blockchain protocols and recent results. It focused on a novel protocol, Colordag (https://eprint.iacr.org/202 2/308), which achieves a strict Nash Equilibrium with high probability.

The conference also included a tutorial on "Serverless Computing: State of the Art and Research Challenges" presented by Karim Djemame, which is summarised in the second invited paper that is included in these proceedings of GECON.

Finally, the conference hosted the workshop WEGreen (SWForum and HUB4CLOUD Workshop on Engineering Green and Sustainable Software in the Computing Continuum), which was held on September 15th, 2022. The program co-chairs of the workshop were Elisabetta Di Nitto (Politecnico di Milano), Giovanni Rimassa (CIO, Martel Innovate), and David Wallom (University of Oxford).

Finally, we would like to wholeheartedly thank the reviewers and program committee members for completing their reviews on time, giving insightful and valuable feedback to the authors. And we thank Springer for their support in publishing these proceedings.

September 2022

José Ángel Bañares
Jörn Altmann
Orna Agmon Ben-Yehuda
Karim Djemame
Vlado Stankovski
Bruno Tuffin

Organization

Executive Committee

Conference Chair

Vlado Stankovski   University of Ljubljana, Slovenia

Conference Vice-chairs

Karim Djemame   University of Leeds, UK
Orna Agmon Ben-Yehuda   University of Haifa, Israel
Jörn Altmann   Seoul National University, South Korea
José Ángel Bañares   Zaragoza University, Spain
Bruno Tuffin   Inria, France
Maurizio Naldi   Libera Università Maria SS. Assunta Lumsa, Italy

Public Relations Chair

José Ángel Bañares   Zaragoza University, Spain

Program Chairs

Bruno Tuffin   Inria, France
Orna Agmon Ben-Yehuda   University of Haifa, Israel

Special Sessions and Tutorial Chair

Jörn Altmann   Seoul National University, South Korea

Program Committee

Alvaro Arenas   IE University, Spain
Unai Arronategui   University of Zaragoza, Spain
Ashraf Bany Mohamed   University of Jordan, Jordan
Stefano Bistarelli   Università di Perugia, Italy
Rajkumar Buyya   University of Melbourne, Australia

Lutz Schubert	University of Ulm, Germany
Arun Sen	Arizona State University, USA
Jun Shen	University of Wollongong, Australia
Dongnyok Shim	Konkuk University, South Korea
Aleksander Slominski	IBM, USA
Burkhard Stiller	University of Zurich, Switzerland
Djamshid Sultanov	Seoul National University, South Korea
Stefan Tai	TU Berlin, Germany
Thanasis Papaioannou	Athens University of Economics and Business, Greece
Rafael Tolosana-Calasanz	University of Zaragoza, Spain
Iraklis Varlamis	Harokopio University of Athens, Greece
Luis Veiga	Universidade de Lisboa, Portugal
Claudiu Vinte	Bucharest University of Economic Studies, Romania
Carl Waldspurger	Carl Waldspurger Consulting, USA
Stefan Wesner	University of Ulm, Germany
Muhammad Zakarya	Abdul Wali Khan University Mardan, Pakistan
Dimitrios Zissis	University of the Aegean, Greece

Subreviewers

Moysis Symeonidis	University of Cyprus, Cyprus
Joanna Georgiou	University of Cyprus, Cyprus
Mohammed Mubarkoot	Seoul National University, South Korea
Yodit Gebrealif	Seoul National University, South Korea
Jacopo Massa	University of Pisa, Italy
Sebastian Werner	TU-Berlin, Germany

Steering Committee

Karim Djemame	University of Leeds, UK
Jörn Altmann	Seoul National University, South Korea
Jose Ángel Bañares	Zaragoza University, Spain
Orna Agmon Ben-Yehuda	Technion, Israel
Steven Miller	Singapore Management University, Singapore
Omer F. Rana	Cardiff University, UK
Gheorghe Cosmin Silaghi	Babes-Bolyai University, Romania
Konstantinos Tserpes	Harokopio University of Athens, Greece
Maurizio Naldi	Università di Roma, Italy

Contents

Special GECON Topics

The Curation, Interfacing and Analysis Lifecycle of Blockchain Application Data

Ian J. Taylor[1,2]([⊠]) [iD]

[1] SIMBA Chain, South Bend, IN 46617, USA
ian@simbachain.com
[2] University of Notre Dame, Notre Dame, IN 46556, USA

Abstract. This paper discusses the lifecycle of data for next generation Web3 decentralized applications, describing how data can be specified, curated, and analyzed. The focus of this work is to study the different types of approaches for indexing blockchain data in a way that application data and relationships can be designed, retained and exposed. Blockchain transactions conform to smart contracts definitions, which can have inherent structures through standards such as NFTs, but can also be designed in a custom way for bespoke use cases. Existing Web3 approaches either focus on service-based approaches that build custom pipelines that extract data in a specific way, or by creating indexes after data has been written without prior influence on how that data should be consumed. SIMBA Chain is a platform that simplifies the management of a Web3 application's lifecycle and takes an alternative approach by enabling design-time specification of transaction interrelationships. SIMBA enables smart contracts to annotate data relationships between smart contract methods to effectively enable schemas to be defined a priori within the source code. By using these relationships, it then autogenerates a GraphQL schema for convenient consumption. We discuss the pros and cons of such an approach and present three application use cases in coffee tracking, NFT car titles and a supply chain scenario, where the approach was extended to also connect and search data across multiple blockchains.

Keywords: Blockchain · Indexing · We3 · Decentralized · Analytics

1 Introduction

Fundamentally, blockchain's enable a decentralized mechanism for the recording of non-repudiable transactions so that no single entity has control of the data. This is achieved using a distributed consensus algorithm that results in immutable data, making it impossible for data to be tampered with once written. Ethereum [1] is an example of such a blockchain which has a network of Ethereum Virtual Machine (EVM) connected nodes. Transactions are coordinated using smart contracts, written in solidity, which define a data and logic interface to the underlying ledger.

In general, blockchain is the first technology that supports a decentralized point-to-point transition of any digital asset (token) from one entity (or state) to another without

J. Á. Bañares et al. (Eds.): GECON 2022, LNCS 13430, pp. 3–14, 2023.
https://doi.org/10.1007/978-3-031-29315-3_1

using a central coordinator. While cryptocurrency uses this to transfer monetary value, there are many other use cases where support for unhackable transitions of assets is game changing. Smart contracts and NFTs (ERC721 [2]) can be used to digitally track data assets (e.g. IP, legal documents, players in a game) or real world assets (e.g. supply chain, healthcare) to secure and/or optimize business processes. NFTs, for example, can provide digital proof of ownership for anything we own or interact with. Therefore, blockchain is suited where multi-step transactions need verification and traceability.

There have been a plethora of applications deployed on public blockchains, e.g. [3], in the past several years and consequently the capability of analyzing this data has emerged as an important topic of research. However, there is a high overhead to enter into this space because blockchains encode data and the encoded data has meaning that can only be understood if you also understand the smart contract that was used to write it [4]. Therefore, even to read data, significant technical barriers have to be overcome. Over and above this, smart contracts define the behavior of the application, and also define the implicit data relationships between blockchain transactions which store the application's state. However, these relationships are not explicitly defined by a custom application. Of course standardized smart contracts have defined behaviors e.g. mint, transfer for an NFT, but beyond those standards it becomes extremely difficult to extract those relationships automatically. As we will discuss, existing approaches use manual curators or custom analysis to extract the data in a way that is usable for analytics.

In this paper, we will review some of different types of approaches for indexing data and compare it with the approach taken by SIMBA chain [5], which takes a more proactive stance by enabling developers to explicitly ingrain those relationships into their smart contracts so that a schema for extraction can be automatically constructed for querying. We discuss this approach in detail and outline its advantages and disadvantages. We then provide three practical real-world use case examples where this technique has been used.

The rest of the paper is organized as follows. The next section discusses existing Web3 indexing approaches. Section 3 provides a background on SIMBA chain and Sect. 4 describes the indexing approach that it takes. Section 5 provides three real-world use examples that make use of this approach, including tracking bags of coffee in Mexico, managing car titles and registrations using NFTs, and a multi-chain supply chain scenario where an extended relationship graph enables search across these chains. Section 6 provides a future view for this research area and Sect. 7 concludes. Section 8 acknowledges colleagues that contributed to SIMBA Chain.

2 Web3 Indexing Approaches

One of the key needs for next-generation Web3 applications is to index and consume Web3 data so that full provenance traces can be queried for each asset across its lifecycle. For cryptocurrency, this is reasonably straightforward because standard interfaces are exposed for transferring tokens, which can be captured to extract transactions between different wallets. However, even in this case, on-chain data needs to be decoded according to the smart contract interfaces to recreate machine readable dataset for analysis. Furthermore, some applications have tens of smart contracts interacting in complex ways with complex data relationships between methods and contracts. To analyze data there are two overarching approaches:

- **After the fact:** where schemas are built and data is indexed after data is stored on a blockchain, without pre-chain design strategies.
- **Before the fact:** where relationships and schemas are built beforehand, perhaps into the source code, before data is stored on the blockchain.

For the first category there are many companies that offer consultancy services providing customized datasets for Web3 applications. Chainalysis [6] is one such popular service that operates in this way but there are many more. However, extracting information from a blockchain is not new, with efforts starting as soon as the difficulties of parsing the blockchain's structure became apparent. Early initiatives, such as EtherQL [7], attempted to provide an efficient query layer for Ethereum, for analyzing blockchain data, including the ability to perform range queries and top-k queries, which can be integrated with other applications.

A notable and more recent example in the Web3 community is "TheGraph" [9], which provides a decentralized incentivized mechanism for indexing and querying blockchain data. TheGraph makes it possible to query data that is difficult to query directly by enabling curators to create "subgraphs", which define the data TheGraph will index. In other words, curators take time to understand the transactions and how they relate to each other in order to create a GraphQL schema and mapping that others can use. Anyblock [10] is another tool that employs the use of Elasticsearch and PostgreSQLto support to search, filter and aggregate across multiple Ethereum based blockchains. However, the data would need to be curated and tied together for this to work, so domain knowledge of the structure and purpose of the application would be needed by the curator of this information. A survey of a number of other different methods is provided by Akcora et al. [8], but they all offer after the fact indexing.

3 SIMBA Chain

Incubated at the University of Notre Dame in 2017, SIMBA Chain (short for Simple Blockchain Applications) is an enterprise development platform to bridge and connect to Web3. SIMBA Blocks is the core offering, abstracting the complexities of blockchain development to make Web3 accessible to all. Blocks provides a low-configuration environment that auto-generates REST APIs for smart contracts on multiple blockchain protocols. Developers can choose and migrate between public, private, and hybrid chains, and optimize and future-proof their Web3 applications.

Blocks has 12 components that support and simplify blockchain integration, see Fig. 1. The auth layer wraps the platform to provide bindings to authentication and authorization frameworks, including Auth0, Active Directory and for the DoD, CAC cards. The Blocks model enables a graph of relationships to be created, linking smart contracts, versions and blockchain (see next section). The other components provide enterprise grade tooling for resilient, scalable and sustainable blockchain applications.

SIMBA provides a generic API to multiple blockchain systems so the system does not have a dependency on a single blockchain or distributed ledger technology. SIMBA

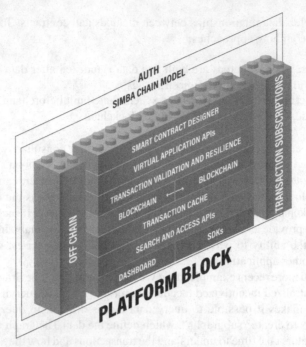

Fig. 1. The components of the SIMBA Chain Platform.

currently supports Ethereum [11], Quorum[12], Hyperledger Fabric[13] and Polygon [14]. It has previously interfaced with Stellar [15], RSK [16], Binance [17], Ava Labs Avalanche [18], Hyperledger Burrow [19] and Hyperledger Sawtooth [20].

Smart contracts can be deployed onto any supported blockchain and an API is generated. Smart contract methods are exposed as REST endpoints using POST and GET with payloads mapping to method parameters, providing a simple, well known interface for developers. APIs are virtual and auto-generated and with no code to manage, Blocks is scalable. APIs are fully documented using Swagger or ReDoc, the Swagger interface being shown in Fig. 2.

Blocks Smart contract method and parameter validation ensures payloads are valid, fixing minor errors and returning major ones before posting to blockchain. Blocks uses an intelligent nonce management mechanism using distributed locking and caching. The chain watcher component uses asynchronous queues and topics, where each transaction can be monitored for completion and trigger further processing such as notifications. When transactions are processed, Blocks adds them to the database Transaction Cache. This rigorous approach ensures resilience and supports lightning fast data search.

Blocks also provides support for off-chaining data. Files attached to a POST are bundled, with each file stored and referenced, using its hashcode, in a manifest file, which is also stored off-chain, with its hashcode stored on the blockchain. The system can retrieve files by using the hashcode to retrieve the manifest, and then using each hashcode to retrieve the files. Currently, SIMBA supports Ceph [21], IPFS [22], Azure

Fig. 2. A Swagger generated interface to the REST API for a smart contract in SIMBA.

Blob Storage [23], Amazon S3 [24], and flat files systems, with further data stores being simple to integrate.

SIMBA Blocks has a sophisticated notification system that can attach triggers to smart contract transactions and notify by email, SMS or using a Web endpoint to connect to other systems. SIMBA supports configurable targets for authentication e.g. SMS, SMTP and filters can be chained to create logic expressions to notify on specific situations e.g. notify if (id = 8756) & (name = Ian). Finally, SDKs make client development simple and streamline client-side transaction signing. SIMBA supports multiple programming languages with SDKs in Python, Java, Node and.NET. This code snippet uses the Node SDK to send a signed data payload to a method on a smart contract hosted on Quorum.

4 SIMBA'S Indexing Approach

As described in Sect. 2, in the Web3 community there are decentralized indexing systems that can be choreographed using data that is already written but there lacks a more proactive design- and implementation-time approach, which can embed data relationships across assets and be used to understand the semantics of the assets across the Web3 application.

The SIMBA Graph Model (SGM) approach is designed to address these issues. Complex relationships within and between assets can be stored using SGM, curated in the smart contracts and then schemas can be automatically generated for complex graph-based querying at consumption. The SIMBA Chain model conceptualizes an application's data and relationships using business process concepts; assets (nouns) represent digital entities and transitions (verbs) representing transitions of assets.

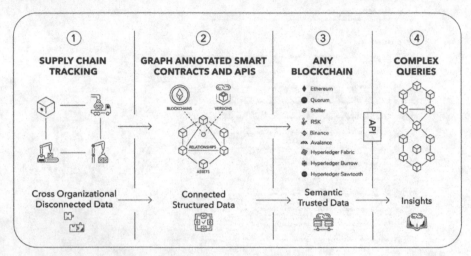

Fig. 3. A supply chain scenario to illustrate how the SIMBA model process works

To illustrate this approach, Fig. 3 shows how a package can be tracked across a supply chain. Using Blocks, the relationships between the package and how it is tracked, shown on the left, are built into smart contracts using annotations and stored on the blockchain. Using these relationships, SIMBA can generate a schema automatically, using GraphQL. This enables application data and their relationships to be defined up front in the code, and queried across those relationships.

This model is used in the Smart Contract Designer (SCD) UI low-code smart contract development environment, and in the dynamic creation of the REST based application-oriented APIs. Using this approach blockchain transactions can be searched using Graph queries. Figure 4 shows an example of this UI being used to create a complex supply chain use case, with the red rectangles representing the assets, the blue ellipses representing transitions and the lines specifying the relationships between assets and assets or assets and their transitions. Each entity can be double clicked to specify the parameters to record at each stage.

The Blocks graph can also represent smart contract versioning; each version is linked with the previous version and forms a queryable graph that can access data from all smart contract versions. Graph links can further connect smart contracts from one blockchain to another. In this way, future proof sustainable blockchain applications can be built, with the graph capturing the application's evolution; one search can potentially traverse the same application co-hosted on several blockchains with multiple smart contract versions.

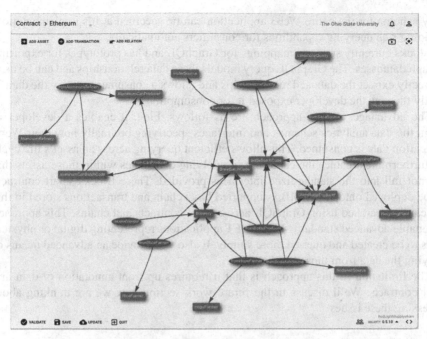

Fig. 4. A supply chain asset graph created in the smart contract designer tool

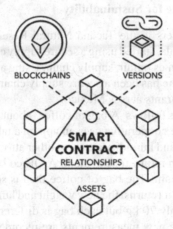

The SGM can be specified using the SCD tool or can be added manually to smart contracts, to enable a coder to specify data relationships within assets, between assets to support far richer asset transition. Furthermore, using the SCD such relationships can used used at a higher level and can be used to specify the smart contract standards to be used e.g. ERC721, along with the asset's data relationships, and SIMBA is capable of generating a template "blocks package", which consists of fully audited ERC721 contracts with inter-asset relationships baked in, meaning that the design level data query schema for the entire Web3 application can be specified at it's implementation, providing rich querying capabilities for consumers automatically.

Blocks currently supports mappings for GraphQL and has prototypes for exporting to graph databases. The GraphQL query models these data relationships and can be used to directly extract the data and relationships and allows a consumer to query the data in exactly the way the developer exposed it for consumption.

The advantages of this approach are as follows. First, it enables a developer to design the data analytics schemas and interfaces specifying optimally how their Web3 application data is consumed. This allows efficient querying across an asset's life cycle and furthermore, enables the capturing of evolving data states within those assets that may not fall into the standardized interfaces provided. These Blocks smart contracts can be deployed onto any SIMBA supported blockchain and transactions stored in this way can be searched using GraphQL across data, contracts and chains. This approach will enable advanced standards-based NFT applications representing digital or physical assets to be created and queried more simply. It also will provide an advanced means of querying the data from those tokens.

The limitation of this approach is that it requires up front annotation of data and smart contracts. We'll discuss in the future work section how we are thinking about addressing these issues.

5 Use Cases

5.1 Tracking Bags of Coffee for Sustainability

In January, 2021, small farmers in the Tacaná Natural Reserve, a volcano biosphere boarding Mexico and Guatemala, started using a secure supply chain. The problem solved was an inefficient, and sometimes unfair, supply chain. Using a blockchain coupled with physical attributes, the outcome has been a secure supply chain from individual farmers to more than 200 Toks Restaurants across Mexico.

The process is described as follows. A bag of coffee (about 100 kg) is delivered from a farm to the cooperative. The cooperative uses an app on a tablet to register the bag of coffee, measuring the weight and humidity amongst other attributes, and then the farmer digitally signs to hand it off in return for payment. A QR code for the bag is generated and registered on the blockchain. The bag of coffee then is sent to the desheller (also registered on chain) and when it returns, the new weight and humidity is measured again. The new weight will be roughly 70 kg but each bag is different. Also, the humidity for each bag will vary too. These new measurements are recorded on the blockchain and associated with the QR code.

This coupling of the physical attributes makes counterfeiting extremely challenging. A counterfeiter cannot simply copy the QR code onto a fake bag of deshelled coffee because it would be very unlikely that the weight and humidity would match. This scheme therefore provides authenticity and a robust anti-counterfeit mechanism. For the restaurant customers, the secure supply chain ensures the coffee is sustainably sourced and for the farmers, this ensures that counterfeit coffee cannot enter into their supply chain.

This tracking of the coffee at different supply chain locations forms the asset (bag of coffee) and transition (how the state of that bag changed) relationships across the supply chain. With SIMBA chain, we capture these relationships and encode them into smart contracts. The result is that TOKs can query the entire provenance of a bag of coffee with a single query, using GraphQL under the hood, which will return every touch point for that bag of coffee across the supply chain.

5.2 Car Titles and Registrations

Tracking automotive sales, resales and titles use archaic paper systems that are riddled with errors and fraud. SIMBA Chain has been working with California auto dealers to track titles across the vehicle life cycle using VIN numbers and tokenization technology.

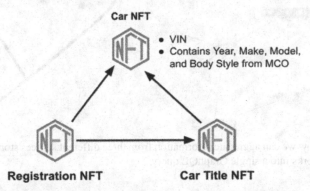

Fig. 5. The three NFTs used to model a car, its title and the registration.

As shown in Fig. 5, we used three NFTs to represent the different components of the application. A car NFT represents the car itself by using the VIN number as the NFT identifier. A car title NFT represents the information of the title but also has a relationship with the car NFT to tie back to the original entity. A registration NFT contains the registration information, which ties back to the car NFT and also references the car title NFT information. This is a simple scenario but it shows how complex relationships can become for real-world applications. Car titles may only need 3 NFTs but if you factor in liens, leases, and so forth it can get more complex. Imagine what an NFT structure for the purchase of a house might look like.

5.3 Supply Chain Across Multiple Blockchains

In supply chains, applications can include tracking parts from creation to installation to ensure their transition across the supply chain is fully traceable and verifiable, to make counterfeiting impossible and ownership, including the origins of those parts, fully transparent. And since a blockchain is immutable, it makes it impossible for anyone, including adversaries, to tamper with the data. Figure 6 shows a supply chain scenario which connects three blockchain networks using the same GraphQL schema interface that we use for the querying of method and contract relationships.

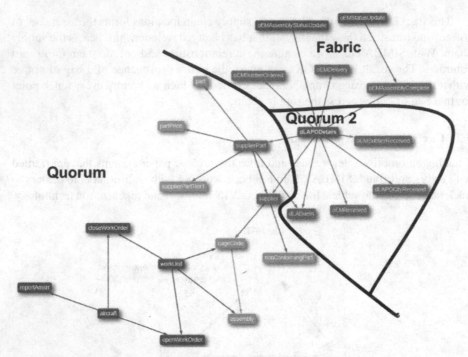

Fig. 6. Shows how we can aggregate information from three different sources stored on different blockchain networks into a single GraphQL query.

To achieve this, we essentially extend the graph to include a connection from a parameter on a contract on one blockchain with a parameter on a contract on another. In the example in Fig. 6, we connect a PO order from one system on Quorum with a PO number on a contract on a supply network on Hyperledger Fabric to track the progress of the production of that part. We then connect the Cage code of the supplier and part to the SupplierPart method on a contract on a further Qurum network to map those to resolvable public data from PUBLOG [25]. This enables us to embed extra part information and supplier details into a single query, just by simply connecting different applications on different chains together.

6 Future Directions

In the future, we imagine far more complex NFT interactions, where each NFT could represent a digital or physical object with evolving internal states as they transition from one state to another; imagine a complex supply chain for an aircraft wing that contains multiple assemblies each having subassemblies, which are each manufactured by a different supply chain tier. Such interactions require complex modeling of the internal data state and how that state impacts other assets as they move around the supply chain. NFTs can represent assemblies and can be linked through to subassembly NFTs to create a structured tracking mechanism for each step of production, and each supply chain tier.

In fact, NFTs in the future could represent anything we own or legally bind ourselves to, from cars, homes, or even, as some suggest, marriage [26], or digital assets like data files, IP usage, or any contractual exchange. NFTs could also represent physical assets by binding physical to digital codes (e.g. RFID, QR Codes, NFC, or image feature prints) tracked using blockchain, to enable the tracking of any physical parts (e.g. wings, tailhooks etc.).

The above approaches provide some underlying techniques for the curation and querying of blockchain relationships. However, GraphQL is not a flexible graph model, it rather provides a schema to access information. This means that multi-level relationships, for example where wallets transact with wallets across several levels, are not possible to implement, because recursion is not supported. What is needed is a full graph database approach that can support recursion to provide the capability of creating a global graph of cryptocurrency and blockchain interactions and relationships.

Another area which we are investigating is the idea of bypassing the annotations for smart contracts and looking at using code inspection to automatically extract relationships or execution trails. This is still under investigation but has the potential to provide the power of the annotation approach without needing to do this manually. If these behaviors can be dynamically built and embedded into a revolving schema, this could provide a more turnkey approach for this in the future.

7 Conclusions

In this paper, we discussed the existing Web3 indexing approaches and compared those with the approach that SIMBA chain takes, offering a "before the fact" model rather than trying to retrospectively retrofit a schema for reading the data. We provided a background into SIMBA and discussed this indexing approach in detail and how it differed from the state of the art. We then provided three real-world use examples that make use of this approach, by illustrating how each benefitted from having a single query to consume the data. These use cases included tracking bags of coffee, managing car titles and registrations using NFTs, and an extended supply chain scenario that uses this approach to enable search across three blochains.

Acknowledgements. Thanks so much to the SIMBA Chain team for realizing the vision of the SIMBA Chain platform and product.

References

1. Wood, G.: Ethereum: a secure decentralised generalised transaction ledger - e94ebda (2018). https://github.com/ethereum/yellowpaper/
2. NFT ERC721 Standard. https://eips.ethereum.org/EIPS/eip-721
3. 34 Blockchain Applications and Real-World Use Cases. https://builtin.com/blockchain/blockchain-applications
4. Brinckman, E., Kuehlkamp, A., Nabrzyski, J., Taylor, I.J.: Techniques and applications for crawling, ingesting and analyzing blockchain data. In: Proceedings of the 2019 International Conference on Information and Communication Technology Convergence (ICTC), pp. 717–722 (2019)

5. SIMBA Chain. http://www.simbachain.com/
6. Chainalysis. https://www.chainalysis.com/
7. Li, Y., Zheng, K., Yan, Y., Liu, Q., Zhou, X.: EtherQL: a query layer for blockchain system. In: Candan, S., Chen, L., Pedersen, T.B., Chang, L., Hua, W. (eds.) DASFAA 2017. LNCS, vol. 10178, pp. 556–567. Springer, Cham (2017). https://doi.org/10.1007/978-3-319-55699-4_34
8. Akcora, C.G., Dixon, M.F., Gel, Y.R., Kantarcioglu, M.: Blockchain data analytics. Intell. Inform. **4** (2018)
9. The Graph Documentation. https://thegraph.com/docs/
10. Any Block Analytics. https://www.anyblockanalytics.com/docs/main/
11. Ethereum. https://ethereum.org/
12. Quorum. https://consensys.net/quorum/
13. Hyperledger Fabric. https://www.hyperledger.org/use/fabric
14. Polygon. https://polygon.technology/
15. Stellar. https://stellar.org/
16. RSK. https://www.rsk.co/
17. Binance Chain. https://www.bnbchain.org/en
18. Ava Labs Avalanche. https://www.avalabs.org/
19. Hyperledger Burrow. https://www.hyperledger.org/project/hyperledger-burrow
20. Hyperledger Sawtooth. https://www.hyperledger.org/use/sawtooth
21. Ceph. https://ceph.io/en/
22. IPFS. https://ipfs.tech/
23. Azure Blob Storage. https://azure.microsoft.com/en-us/products/storage/blobs/
24. Amazon S3. https://aws.amazon.com/s3/
25. PUBLOG. https://www.dla.mil/Information-Operations/Services/Applications/PUB-LOG/
26. How India's First Couple Got Married on the Blockchain. https://www.indiatimes.com/technology/news/india-first-couple-marriage-on-blockchain-561474.html

Serverless Computing: Introduction and Research Challenges

Karim Djemame$^{(\boxtimes)}$ (iD)

School of Computing, University of Leeds, Leeds, UK
K.Djemame@leeds.ac.uk
https://eps.leeds.ac.uk/computing/staff/187/professor-karim-djemame

Abstract. Serverless computing is a technology that offers the ability
to create modular, highly-scalable, fault-tolerant applications, leveraging container-based virtualisation to deploy applications and services. It
is revolutionising the way we think about application development, and
serverless platforms are already ubiquitous in the public and private sec-
tors. Commercial solutions dominate the market with widespread adoption from industry giants such as Amazon, Google and Microsoft, though
open-source solutions do exist such as Apache OpenWhisk, Fission and
OpenFaaS. This tutorial will present the state-of-the-art in serverless
computing research, and provide useful insights into the main challenges
that motivate researchers to work on this topic. It will also identify
research gaps for future research.

Keywords: Serverless computing · Cloud Computing ·
Containerisation · Performance Evaluation

1 Introduction

The goal of serverless computing is to provide isolated environments that
abstract underlying technologies and expose small runtime containers for users
to run functions as code [13]. It provides a resource-efficient, low overhead alternative to Virtual Machines (VMs) and containers. Serverless computing simply
means that the serverless platform allows a developer to build code and deploy
it without ever needing to configure or manage underlying servers. The unit of
deployment is the code; not the container that hosts the code, or the server
that runs the code, but simply the code itself. However, a major requirement for
writing serverless code is the ability to express the logic as *functions* that are
instantiated to process a single event triggered by a service.

With zero infrastructure and maintenance costs and little-to-no operating
expense, a serverless computing platform is an ideal solution to build and optimise any Internet of Things (IoT) operation as it allows IoT businesses to offload
all of a server's typical operational backend responsibilities [20]. Moreover, such
system is a natural fit for edge computing applications as serverless computing also supports the protocols which IoT devices require in actual deployment
conditions.

J. Á. Bañares et al. (Eds.): GECON 2022, LNCS 13430, pp. 15–23, 2023.
https://doi.org/10.1007/978-3-031-29315-3_2

For a map of state-of-the-art research on the topic of FaaS platform and tooling engineering together with analysis of relations of the proposed concepts to existing solutions, the reader is referred to [35]: the mapping study on engineering FaaS platforms and tools provides insights on publication trends, the common challenges and drivers for research as well as information on industry participation in research publications.

2   Service Models

Serverless computing is linked to mainly two service models [35], similar to the ones that originally emerged with the rise of cloud computing:

1. *Backend as a Service(BaaS)*: This refers to services that offer features traditionally implemented by back-end applications such as databases or API servers. Users can incorporate them in their front-end web applications without the provisioning, setup and management of servers [11]. Although similar to Platform as a Service (PaaS), they are more full-featured, implementing server side logic such as user authentication or push/pull notifications which PaaS offerings forego in favor of more flexibility.
2. *Function as a Service(FaaS)*: This model allows users to develop their application logic by compositing event-driven executable elements called functions. These functions are executed inside ephemeral containers, taking advantage of container virtualization to quickly provision resources for the duration of the execution. Most notably these containers are managed by the providers and scale automatically in number based on demand. FaaS is the most prominent model of serverless computing and has seen widespread

3   Commercial Offering

Serverless computing has seen widespread adoption from tech industry giants such as Amazon [1], Microsoft [7] and Google [5]. *Amazon AWS Lambda* is a service for executing stateless functions in the cloud, triggered by events, with transparent provisioning and no infrastructure management from users [1]. It has since grown into one of the most widely used and researched FaaS platforms, as evidenced by the extensive literature on performance evaluation [22] and investigations into its viability in various application domains [18].

Similarly, Microsoft have general availability of their own FaaS service, *Azure Functions*, citing a much wider service-function binding capability, allowing functions to be triggered by events from external services. Azure Functions is built on top of Microsoft's PaaS offering, Azure App Service, and theWebJobs SDK with a runtime layer on top to support multiple programming languages. Google also have *Cloud Functions*, their own brand of serverless, and so does IBM which developed of what would eventually become *OpenWhisk*, the open-source serverless platform that embraces community collaboration. OpenWhisk was released to the general public and admitted into the Apache Foundation and was the basis for IBM's commercial FaaS product, *Cloud Functions*.

4   Open Source Solutions

Serverless computing has also seen adoption from the public domain, with open-source projects like *Apache OpenWhisk* [2], *Fission* [4], *OpenFaas* [8], *IronFunctions* [6] and more.

OpenLambda [21] is an open-source platform for building web services applications using the serverless computing model. OpenWhisk [2] follows a simple event-driven architecture - functions are being triggered in response to events originating from direct invocations to the OpenWhisk API, or external services that are integrated in the platform through specialized packages. These community-developed packages allow functions to be triggered when an external action is being performed, such as when a new commit is pushed to a GitHub repository, or a file has finished uploading to a Dropbox folder. Every action in OpenWhisk is transformed and routed through its RESTful HTTP-based API that serves as the platform's single point of entry.

5   Research Categories

An investigation of the challenges and drivers that motivate researchers to engineer new or extend existing FaaS platforms and platform-specific tools is found in [35]. The state of the art on the topic of developing new or enhancing existing FaaS platforms and tools engineering focuses on the following: 1) Function Execution; 2) Platform deployment environment; 3) Testing and observability; 4) Benchmarking; 5) Costs optimisation; 6) Programming models; 7) Research-centric platforms; 8) Deployment automation; 9) Migration, and 10) Continuous integration/Continuous delivery pipeline.

One of the findings in [35] is that the challenges tackled by researchers are heterogeneous and target different layers of the FaaS platform, with a bulk of the work focusing on optimizing the performance of function execution aspects using various strategies, e.g., optimize or replace function runtime, improve function scheduling and resources allocation.

Moreover, underlying *metrics* that are considered in the literature include [34]:

- *Communication performance*: this is important in function composition, and is particularly used for complex serverless applications such as sequence and nested chain;
- *Startup latency*: although function execution time is usually short, a 15× factor differential is noted between *cold* and *warm* times [26]. To avoid start-up latency, the underlying virtualisation technology must be optimised to decrease the start-up latency of *cold* start and can be tackled by suitable managing of the function instances in the serverless platform, e.g., reusing launched instances by keeping them *warm* for a period of time [25], or reduction of the container image size.

- *Stateless overhead*: serverless functions are by definition stateless. Two options are considered for an application that wants to preserve state across function executions: 1) the state can be fully encapsulated within the event message passing between the function executions. If there are multiple functions executing in a workflow, each function will find the full application state it needs in the event message it receives, operate on it, and pass it on to the next function, and 2) persist state across function executions is to utilise a storage system, e.g. AWS S3.
- *Resource efficiency*: from the platform perspective, this is the ability to co-locate serverless functions with other workloads for utilisation improvement. For users, the aim is to provision resources for Quality of Service and economy benefit.

6   Research Challenges

There are a number of research challenges in serverless computing such as unreliability, large overheads and an absence of benchmarks [16]. Investigations into various aspects of serverless architectures are therefore required to guide the decision making process. In the following, some of these challenges are discussed.

6.1   Performance

There has been extensive research around factors affecting function execution performance [31] as well as some evaluations of commercial and open-source serverless frameworks. A comprehensive evaluation of Apache OpenWhisk is evaluated in [14], with a series of experiments designed and implemented to assess its performance in terms of effectiveness and efficiency. Two metrics were of interest in experimentation: function runtime and resource utilisation. Experiments also involved creation of two alternate solutions used as benchmarks for the results produced by OpenWhisk to provide some context and means for comparison: *Docker* [3] and *native*. The results of experiments showed that OpenWhisk could outperform a solution which employed similar functionality, through use of container-based virtualisation.

Another important point to consider in the context of performance is virtualisation technology. For example, AWS Lambda uses Firecracker micro-VMs [17] which provide enhanced security and workload isolation over traditional VMs, while enabling the speed and resource efficiency of containers.

6.2   Serverless Composition

Serverless applications can be made of multiple functions in a chain, and consequently unreasonable composition may incur high communication overhead. For example, network functions are usually short-lived and in most scenarios, they are chained together to form a Service Function Chain (SFC) [12]. The development and performance tuning of SCFs are difficult and should be considered in designing the more complex application scenarios. Considering serverless parallelism, especially in the context of autoscaling can benefit applications with high efficiency. How to control and manage such parallelism remains an open question.

6.3   Utilisation

Serverless functions are usually scaled up and down on-demand in a serverless platform. Load balancing manages resource utilisation by distributing the function executions to available resources. Function efficiency heavily depends on the resources allocated but at the same time maximising resource utilization is a hard problem, especially in a large scale environment, e.g. cloud computing [34].

As noted previously, an application can be launched as multiple orchestrated functions. To avoid undesired latency and network overhead (and therefore energy consumption), the function executions belonging to the same session can be assigned to the same server. For latency sensitive communication, locality requirements are considered to group functions as a single application.

6.4   Programming Models

Serverless platforms are typically focused on FaaS, where applications need to be redesigned as a set of event-triggered functions implemented in a supported programming language. Consequently, this requires additional effort for the developers as many applications cannot be easily redesigned as a set of functions.

The adoption of serverless computing in Big Data has attracted the attention of researchers and developers. Examples of data analytics over serverless platforms are found in [19] to perform data processing with Spark over Apache OpenWhisk Ooso is an open source tool based on managed cloud services, Amazon S3 and AWS Lambda that allows running MapReduce jobs in a serverless way [29]. Another open-source framework for building serverless applications is AWS Serverless Application Model (SAM) [10] which provides shorthand syntax to express functions, APIs, databases, and event source mappings as well as application modelling using YAML. A programming model designed to create highly-parallel event-driven file-processing serverless applications for serverless architectures is presented in [28]. This programming model allows the user to run generic applications, including legacy ones, on serverless platforms.

6.5   Energy Efficiency

Applications' performance lies with not only efficient node-level execution but energy consumption as well as these applications, e.g. IoT, may operate in a low energy computing environment. A serverless platform does not take into account energy savings in resource management decisions, and therefore addressing performance concerns combined with availability and energy efficiency concerns in serverless computing becomes important.

Serverless platform can be extended to support resource mapping and load balancing to increase resource utilisation by distributing the function executions to available resources with the aim to minimise power consumption. A load balancing strategy should consider functions interactions by assigning the function executions belonging to the same session to the same server. Latency sensitive communication services require careful placement of functions by allowing locality requirements for grouping functions as a single application. Containers image sizes are reduced to speed up the start of a function execution thus avoiding cold start.

The work in [24] proposes RAEF, a function-level runtime system for allocating the resources required by serverless functions in order to minimize power consumption, and which consists of predictors, resource explorer, monitor and coordinator. The work in [12] describes a modular, and micro-service based Software Defined Network (SDN) architecture that applies network programmability within the context of Network Function Virtualisation (NFV) and explores how it could benefit from the serverless computing paradigm. Experimental results show that the serverless paradigm can decrease service latency for disaggregated architectures, and also provide on-demand and scalable resource management. The reduction in the execution time and the average resource usage of microservices allows for many optimizations from the resource management point of view. Follow-up work addresses performance concerns combined with energy efficiency support in serverless computing [9]. To this aim, a number of experiments are conducted to compare the power consumption of a serverless platform, OpenFaaS, against Docker containers with the consideration of applications and benchmarks, driven by SDN and NFV requirements. The experimental results show that OpenFaaS is more power efficient than Docker when the processor and memory are under stress.

6.6   Language Runtimes

One of the most detrimental factors affecting performance in serverless architectures is the notion of cold start that takes place when the first incoming request to an application leads to a time-consuming allocation of resources which delays the response and leads to bad user experience [11]. Research has shown that the choice of language runtime plays a non-trivial role in the performance of serverless applications. In particular, the cold start times differ significantly across different languages and platforms [15]. Various papers have investigated the performance impact the choice of language runtime has on function execution as well as measured runtime overhead through the consideration of different use cases, e.g. a performance and cost analysis of language choice on AWS Lambda and Azure Functions [23]; a just-in-time dynamic language outperforming the compiled alternatives [27]; identification of factors influencing function performance, interpreted languages, effect of cold and warm start [32]; effect of resource provisioning and how it affects performance on commercial platforms (AWS Lambda, Azure, Google Functions) [33]; and comparison of dynamic and compiled languages [30].

Some areas for further research include: 1) the evaluation of more trigger types for invoking functions (e.g. database updates, timers, message queues); 2) the evaluation of additional serverless platforms (e.g. Knative, OpenFaaS, Kubeless and Iron Functions), and 3) the investigation custom runtimes when serverless platforms offer the ability for a custom executable to be used as a runtime environment.

7 Conclusion

This paper has introduced Serverless Computing, a cloud computing model where the exact amount of resources needed by applications is dynamically allocated on-demand. Function-as-a-service (FaaS) is the service model that allows developers to run code directly in the cloud without the need to build packages or maintain any infrastructure. The paper has surveyed and elaborated the research domains in the serverless context and provided useful insights into the main challenges that motivate researchers to work on this topic.

Acknowledgements. The author would like to thank the Next Generation Internet Program for Open INTErnet Renovation (NGI-Pointer 2) for supporting this work under contract 871528 (EDGENESS Project).

References

1. Amazon Web Services. AWS Lambda (2019). https://aws.amazon.com/lambda/
2. Apache Openwhisk. Open Source Serverless Cloud Platform (2010). https://openwhisk.apache.org/
3. Docker. Empowering App Development for Developers (2019). http://www.docker.com
4. Fission - Open source, Kubernetes-native Serverless Framework (2019). https://fission.io
5. Google. Google Cloud Functions (2019). https://cloud.google.com/functions
6. IronFunctions - Open Source Serverless Computing (2019). https://open.iron.io/
7. Microsoft Azure. Azure Functions (2019). https://azure.microsoft.com/en-us/services/functions/
8. OpenFaaS - Serverless Functions, Made Simple (2021). https://openfaas.com/
9. Alhindi, A., Djemame, K., Banaie, F.: On the power consumption of serverless functions: an evaluation of openFaaS. In: Proceedings of the 15th IEEE/ACM International Conference on Utility and Cloud Computing (UCC 2022), Vancouver, Washington. IEEE (2022)
10. Amazon: AWS Serverless Application Model (AWS SAM) (2022). https://github.com/awslabs/serverless-application-model
11. Baldini, I., et al.: Serverless computing: current trends and open problems. CoRR abs/1706.03178 (2017)
12. Banaie, F., Djemame, K.: A serverless computing platform for software defined networks. In: Baares, J., et al. (eds.) GECON 2022. LNCS, pp. 113–123. Springer, Cham (2023)

13. Castro, P., Ishakian, V., Muthusamy, V., Slominski, A.: Serverless programming (function as a service). In: 2017 IEEE 37th International Conference on Distributed Computing Systems (ICDCS), pp. 2658–2659 (2017)
14. Djemame, K., Parker, M., Datsev, D.: Open-source serverless architectures: an evaluation of apache OpenWhisk. In: 2020 IEEE/ACM 13th International Conference on Utility and Cloud Computing (UCC), pp. 329–335 (2020)
15. Djemame, K., Datsev, D., Kelefouras, V.I.: Evaluation of language runtimes in open-source serverless platforms. In: van Steen, M., Ferguson, D., Pahl, C. (eds.) Proceedings of the 12th International Conference on Cloud Computing and Services Science, CLOSER 2022, Online Streaming, 27–29 April 2022, pp. 123–132. SCITEPRESS (2022)
16. van Eyk, E., Iosup, A.: Addressing performance challenges in serverless computing. In: Proceedings of ICT.OPEN 2018, Amersfoort, The Netherlands. ACM (2018)
17. Firecracker: Firecracker: Secure and fast microVMs for serverless computing (2021). https://firecracker-microvm.github.io/
18. Giménez-Alventosa, V., Moltó, G., Caballer, M.: A framework and a performance assessment for serverless MapReduce on AWS Lambda. Future Gener. Comput. Syst. **97**, 259–274 (2019). http://www.sciencedirect.com/science/article/pii/S0167739X18325172
19. Glikson, A.: Transit: flexible pipeline for IoT data with bluemix and openwhisk (2018). https://goo.gl/ThN2TR
20. Großmann, M., Ioannidis, C., Le, D.T.: Applicability of serverless computing in fog computing environments for IoT scenarios. In: Proceedings of the 12th IEEE/ACM International Conference on Utility and Cloud Computing Companion, UCC 2019, pp. 29–34. Companion, Association for Computing Machinery, New York (2019)
21. Hendrickson, S., Sturdevant, S., Harter, T., Venkataramani, V., Arpaci-Dusseau, A.C., Arpaci-Dusseau, R.H.: Serverless computation with openlambda. In: Proceedings of the 8th USENIX Conference on Hot Topics in Cloud Computing, HotCloud 2016, pp. 33–39. USENIX Association, USA (2016)
22. Jackson, D., Clynch, G.: An investigation of the impact of language runtime on the performance and cost of serverless functions. In: 2018 IEEE/ACM International Conference on Utility and Cloud Computing Companion (UCC Companion), pp. 154–160 (2018)
23. Jackson, D., Clynch, G.: An investigation of the impact of language runtime on the performance and cost of serverless functions. In: 2018 IEEE/ACM International Conference on Utility and Cloud Computing Companion, pp. 154–160 (2018)
24. Jia, X., Zhao, L.: RAEF: energy-efficient resource allocation through energy fungibility in serverless. In: 2021 IEEE 27th International Conference on Parallel and Distributed Systems (ICPADS), pp. 434–441. IEEE (2021)
25. Li, Z., Guo, L., Cheng, J., Chen, Q., He, B., Guo, M.: The serverless computing survey: a technical primer for design architecture. ACM Comput. Surv. **54** (2022)
26. Lloyd, W., Ramesh, S., Chinthalapati, S., Ly, L., Pallickara, S.: Serverless computing: an investigation of factors influencing microservice performance. In: 2018 IEEE International Conference on Cloud Engineering (IC2E), pp. 159–169 (2018)
27. Manner, J., Endreß, M., Heckel, T., Wirtz, G.: Cold start influencing factors in function as a service. In: 2018 IEEE/ACM International Conference on Utility and Cloud Computing Companion (UCC Companion), pp. 181–188 (2018)
28. Pérez, A., Moltó, G., Caballer, M., Calatrava, A.: A programming model and middleware for high throughput serverless computing applications. In: Proceedings of the 34th ACM/SIGAPP Symposium on Applied Computing, SAC 2019, pp. 106–113. ACM, New York (2019)

29. Platform, DOS: Ooso: Serverless MapReduce (2017). https://github.com/d2si-oss/ooso

30. Sbarski, P., Cui, Y., Nair, A.: Serverless Architectures on AWS. Manning, 2nd edn. (2022)

31. Scheuner, J., Leitner, P.: Function-as-a-service performance evaluation: a multivocal literature review. J. Syst. Softw. **170**, 110708 (2020)

32. Vojta, R.: AWS journey - API gateway & Lambda & VPC performance (2016). https://www.zrzka.dev/aws-journey-api-gateway-lambda-vpc-performance/

33. Wang, L., Li, M., Zhang, Y., Ristenpart, T., Swift, M.: Peeking behind the curtains of serverless platforms. In: Proceedings of the 2018 USENIX Conference on USENIX Annual Technical Conference, USENIX ATC 2018, pp. 133–145. USENIX Association, USA (2018)

34. Yu, T., et al.: Characterizing serverless platforms with serverlessbench. In: Proceedings of the 11th ACM Symposium on Cloud Computing (SOCC 2020), pp. 30–44. ACM, New York (2020)

35. Yussupov, V., Breitenbücher, U., Leymann, F., Wurster, M.: A systematic mapping study on engineering function-as-a-service platforms and tools. In: Proceedings of the 12th IEEE/ACM International Conference on Utility and Cloud Computing, Auckland, New Zealand (2019)

Business Models, Service Discovery

A Business Model for Multi-tiered Decentralized Software Frameworks: The Case of ONTOCHAIN

Thanasis Papaioannou[✉] and George D. Stamoulis

Athens University of Economics and Business (AUEB), Athens, Greece
{pathan,gstamoul}@aueb.gr

Abstract. Open source licensing enables the inception of collective building of integrated decentralized software frameworks. However, when individual constituents of such a framework are built by independent companies where each of them has its own business plan, then the joint exploitation of the overall software framework becomes very complicated. In this paper, we address this problem, by studying in depth the special case of the joint exploitation of the ONTOCHAIN (OC) blockchain-based software framework that is being built by many companies, each having its own business agenda. We define the business model of OC, whereby the management and maintenance of the jointly-built platform is assumed to be undertaken by a new venture; this offers the platform for dApp (decentralized application) deployment and as a PaaS for development and testing of dApps. We study carefully the business models of all stakeholders in the OC ecosystem and analyze them as a part of the overall value network. Based on realistic revenue and cost parameter assumptions, and analyzing concurrently the business models of all stakeholders in this ecosystem, we establish that win-win outcomes are economically sustainable, provided that revenue sharing is properly coordinated.

Keywords: blockchain · incentive compatibility · economic sustainability · techno-economic analysis · open-source · revenue sharing

1 Introduction

Collectively built integrated decentralized software frameworks can emerge through open-source licensing schemes, e.g., Apache v2.0. However, the business viability of a common platform, when its individual constituents are built by independent companies or individuals with different -often conflicting- business interests, is complicated [5] and even counter-intuitive.

In this paper[1], we address this problem by studying in depth the special case of the joint exploitation of the ONTOCHAIN (OC) blockchain-based software framework [8] that is being built by a large number of individual companies,

---

[1] This work has been funded by the EU project ONTOCHAIN (grant no. 957338).

each having a different business agenda. Based on a well-founded methodology, we define the business model of OC. The management and maintenance of the OC platform is assumed to be undertaken by a new venture, which offers the platform for dApp deployment and as a PaaS for development and testing of dApps. Different service components and library providers on top of the OC platform are assumed to be separate stakeholders with independent business models. The interactions of the OC venture with all other stakeholders in the OC ecosystem are clearly defined in a value network. The business models of all stakeholders in the OC ecosystem have been carefully studied and analyzed. Then, by means of economic sustainability analysis based on realistic revenue and cost parameter assumptions, and based on concurrent analysis of the business models of all stakeholders in this ecosystem, we establish that win-win outcomes for all involved stakeholders in ecosystem are viable and likely to emerge. Finally, we argue that choices regarding revenue sharing in this ecosystem have to be carefully made for the economic robustness of all stakeholders involved, and thus some common understanding and coordination on the exploitation of the OC ecosystem has been found to be of utmost importance.

2   Methodology

To define, describe, select and assess the most promising business model(s) (BM) for OC, we follow the methodology, named *process modelling* [2], as follows: In step 1, market analysis concerns the overview of the global and European blockchain markets in terms of market value per region and per vertical, to overview the current stakeholders in the market, and to investigate existing business paradigms and models. Step 2 is about defining and describing a business model by means of a value network definition and a business model canvas. The value network (VN) concept originates from Michael Porter's well-known value chain concept [9], which is widely used in the business literature to describe the value producing activities of an organization. The concept has been expanded in [1] to include non-linear interactions between one or more enterprises, its customers, suppliers and strategic partners. The Business Model Canvas [7] is considered an established way for describing and visualising business models, by describing the rationale of how an organization creates, delivers and captures value. In step 3, the value network defined in step 2 is analyzed to expose all values exchanged in the interactions of the different roles. These values may include multiple revenue or cost parameters that have to be thoroughly explored. Finally, in step 4, an economic analysis is performed of the proposed business model for a certain time horizon, aiming to answer questions on the profitability of the investment, on its payback period, on its deficits, etc. based on realistic assumption on the various revenue and cost parameters found in step 3.

3   Blockchain Market Overview and Related Work

3.1   The Blockchain Market

The blockchain technology [6] is now recognized as a highly disruptive technology in various sector of the economy, such as monetary transactions, energy, mobility, logistics, supply chain, healthcare and insurance, etc. It is an open, immutable, distributed ledger that acts as a universal depository of all transactions between involved parties. Modern blockchains, as initiated by Ethereum [10], enable the specification of advanced logic and the automation of business workflows to be executed within blockchain transactions in the form of smart contracts to ensure resistance to censorship and tampering, pseudo-anonymity, fault-tolerance, resilience, and non-repudiation. The global blockchain technology market size is now exploding. According to Grand View Research[2], the global blockchain technology market size was valued at USD 3.67 billion in 2020 and it is expected to expand at a compound annual growth rate (CAGR) of 82.4% from 2021 to 2028.

3.2 Business Models in Blockchain

Here, we overview some of the most important business models[3] to exploit blockchain-based technological solutions.

– **Token Economy – Tokenomics:** In this business model, which is the most common one, a utility token is employed to exchange goods and services through blockchain transactions, or to perform activities in the blockchain network. The blockchain platform issues this utility token and the end-users can acquire it either in exchange of FIAT money or as rewards for performing some useful work for the network, e.g., in Ethereum (v1.0), Bitcoin, Ravencoin, etc., miners are offered tokens as incentives for validating the blockchain transactions. Moreover, kickstarting blockchains ventures often involves an initial coin offering (ICO) where a portion of the utility tokens is sold to the community for fund raising, while the rest is held by the ventures.
– **Blockchain as a service:** This business model involves the provision of a platform for other businesses to use blockchain technology for doing their business. Microsoft(Azure), Amazon(AWS), IBM(BlueMix), etc. offer blockchain as a service(BaaS).
– **Development Platforms:** In this business model, blockchain infrastructure is offered as a platform (i.e., libraries, IDE, etc.) for development of blockchain software, such as decentralized applications (dApps) or services, e.g., Hyperledger Fabric [3]. Contrary to the BaaS model, dApps and services cannot be deployed on top of these platforms for production purposes.
– **Blockchain-based software products:** This is a business model where software companies develop blockchain solutions and then sell them to bigger companies. There is a reasonable payment upfront for the blockchain software, while support fees are usual.
– **Network fee charge:** In this business model, a corporate maintains a blockchain platform with non-trivial functionality where third-party decentralized applications (dApps) can be deployed and execute. The corporate

---

[2] https://www.grandviewresearch.com/industry-analysis/blockchain-technology-market.
[3] https://101blockchains.com.

takes care of infrastructure costs as well as operational expenses for the third-party dApps to run, and charges dApp providers a (network) fee, e.g., Ethereum or Neo.

- **Blockchain Consulting:** This business model involves the provision of training for consulting services around the blockchain technology, e.g., by Deloitte, IBM or others.
- **P2P Services Exchange:** This business model is similar to that of the Network Fee Charge, in the sense that the blockchain platform is offered to third party dApps to run. However, in this case it is envisioned that in these dApps services are exchanged among end users in a P2P manner. A portion of the service fees paid by the end-users is supposed to be withheld by the blockchain platform that hosts the services.

The effect that blockchain technologies can have on each element of the business model canvas has been outlined in [4]. Blockchain can enable reach of additional customer segments, facilitate (faster) transactions with previously unreachable customers or ones that were expensive to reach. As established in [5] only few multi-tiered platforms, such as ONTOCHAIN (OC), are managed effectively, so that competing and conflicting forces are balanced and intra-competition is minimized; the governance is of key importance, i.e., involving decision rights and accountability to encourage desirable behavior in the use of the platform. In OC, we employ a hybrid business model that combines P2P services exchange and the network fees, while we strongly emphasize in achieving win-win outcomes in a fully transparent way, as explained in the following section.

4   The Business Model

ONTOCHAIN (OC) offers a technological framework for a human-centered Internet, based on decentralization of power and privacy. Furthermore, the end users are going to benefit from democratic, transparent and credible mechanisms. This project aims to achieve a common path of Semantic Web and Blockchain by delivering software for reliable, traceable and transparent ontological knowledge management. To this end, we develop a blockchain platform that will offer functionality on self-sovereign identities, credentials-based authentication, semantic annotation and storage of blockchain transactions and smart contracts, decentralized oracles, decentralized reputation systems, privacy-aware data processing, copyrights management, and more, as SDKs and APIs for innovative decentralized apps (dApps) that support our vision for more trustworthy services exchange and content handling, and more privacy-friendly, decentralized Internet where people will feel more empowered. We develop a blockchain network infrastructure on top of Ethereum that will be able to host these dApps and support the execution of their smart contracts.

The OC software platform is being currently developed by third-party subprojects selected in the OC open calls, according to the requirements, the overall architectural design defined by the OC consortium and subject to mentoring provided by the OC core partners. The OC infrastructure (i.e., the blockchain network) is built mainly by volunteering resource contributions by OC core members and OC third-party subproject teams. While limiting ownership of blockchain nodes the OC ecosystem, as explained above, we do consider blockchain network expansion according to the computational needs of the dApps deployed on top of the OC platform, as explained in Sect. 7. Opening up the blockchain network to the public and the respective incentive scheme are left for future work.

Thus, so far, the creation of the initial ecosystem of OC has been funded by the EU. However, supporting the OC blockchain network in the future and sustaining its development will incur significant capital and operational expenses, e.g., for software maintenance and upgrade, for electricity, for network administration, etc. The plan is that OC in the future is run by a joint venture, henceforth referred to as *OC venture* created by the OC core members. OC third-party subprojects, referred to as *OC Service Components*, will be invited to sign a joint exploitation agreement for their solutions with the OC venture in mutually favorable terms. The joint exploitation agreement has to involve a procedure for governance and decision making in the OC network and may appoint a special committee for this purpose, similarly to the NEO council or the Ethereum foundation. Note that all different stakeholders in the OC ecosystem have their individual business interests and that there is no governing force dictating any business relation or coalition. Therefore, any envisioned business interaction should be incentive compatible for all involved stakeholders.

Two main business use cases (BUCs) are envisioned for the OC venture (see Fig. 1a):

- BUC1: Offering a platform for the deployment and execution of innovative dApps, which are then later exchanged among producers and consumers in a P2P manner.
- BUC2: Offering a platform for the development and testing of innovative dApps to developers and software companies.

These BUCs do not differ significantly and therefore they are considered jointly in the sequel. We will employ a combination of the P2P exchanges platform and the network fees business models described in Sect. 3.2. We envision that the OC platform will withhold a certain fraction of the fees of the services exchanged in the platform, provided that these services utilize the functionality and the resources of the platform. This choice is supported by the fact that the utilization of OC functionality and resources incur costs (e.g., computational, personnel, electricity, etc.) that need to be paid. Moreover, we envision that the OC ventures charges network fees for the deployment of dApps on the platform and/or the utilization of platform resources for development and testing purposes. The deployment of dApps by *dApp providers*, is associated to the allocation of scarce resources, e.g., storage, server capacity, etc., while development and testing (similar to service transactions) by *dApp developers* consume computational resources. OC Service Components are business entities that provide core functionality to the OC platform, such as privacy-aware data processing, reputation management, self-sovereign identities and so on [8]. Many have developed in the open calls of OC, but more may be developed and offered within OC platform in the future. An OC Service Component may make available its

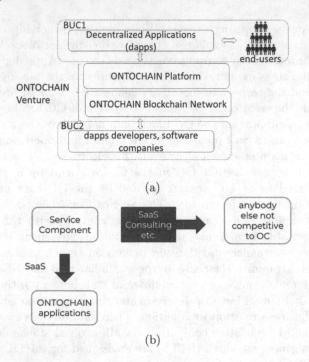

Fig. 1. (a) OC main BUCs, (b) Business model for an OC Service Component.

services through hardware infrastructure (e.g., server nodes), additional to the OC blockchain network, which will involve capital investments. Moreover, each dApp utilizing the functionality of one or more service components will incur costs associated to the resource utilization of the respective service components. Therefore, it is envisioned that part of the total dApp service and network fees withheld by the OC platform is given to the various service components utilized by the dApp. A service component may offer its functionality to the OC platform (and subsequently to the dApp deployed on top of the latter) or any other entity that is not directly competitive to the value proposition of OC. A high-level view of the business model of a service component is depicted in Fig. 1b.

5   Value Proposition, Revenue Streams

Out of the business model canvas analysis, we will focus only on the value proposition and the revenue streams for brevity reasons. Value proposition of ONTOCHAIN (OC) can be defined in qualitative or quantitative terms. The trustworthy service/data transactions, the data/user privacy, the semantic richness of blockchain data and the trustworthiness of data and entities belong to the qualitative value proposition. The quantitative part refers to rewards for involved stakeholders, especially to service component providers and blockchain nodes, to profit prospects for dApp developers, dApp providers and investors, and to increased net benefit (i.e., utility) for end users of the dApps deployed at the OC platform. In general, it is related to the profitability and economic viability of the OC ecosystem as a whole with the profit or the prosperity exceeding the operating costs in terms of electricity consumption or otherwise, so that there is a significant return on investment (ROI) and a short payback period.

Overall, OC will follow a SaaS/PaaS business paradigm, with the following revenue streams for its constituents (i.e., OC venture, OC Service Components, OC nodes):

1. OC offers the libraries and the platform/resources for dApp developers/ dApp providers to build and deploy their services. One-off, subscription fees and/or transaction fees will be used.
2. End-users subscribe/pay per use the dApp providers for dApp transactions. Part of the transaction fee is given to OC and part is given to the different libraries/solution providers (i.e., Third-Party Service Components) that are used by the dApp. Additional fees for data employed within the dApps are paid to Data Providers.
3. OC pays blockchain nodes with gas fees for their computational resources employed in the operation of the OC platform.

6   The Value Network

Next, we describe the business interactions and the value exchanged among the different entities of the ONTOCHAIN (OC) ecosystem, i.e., the value network of OC depicted in Fig. 2. The *OC venture* (i) provides support, visibility and funding to *OC Service Components* (i.e., core software contributors) that invites through OC open calls; (ii) provides network and platform to *dApp Providers* for some fee to *dApp providers* and/or *dApp developers*; (iii) encapsulates Platform Components that share (part of) the value inserted into the system by *End-Users* and *dApp Providers*. The *OC Service Providers* (i) contribute pieces or service components of the OC platform in exchange of funding; (ii) may receive additional income when different dApps employ their specific components (may be subject to exclusivity agreement), which is based on the exploitation agreement with the OC platform and it can be subscription-based or usage-based. The *dApp providers* (i) offer dApps to end-users for a fee; (ii) pay the *OC venture* for hosting their apps; (iii) pay for the *OC Service Components* and the computational resources that their dApp consumes when it is offered to end-users; (iv) pay the *dApp developers* for software and support. The *dApp developers* (i) work on the development of decentralized applications and the protocols that will govern them and get paid by *dApp providers*; (ii) may offer support services to *dApp providers*; (iii) may pay the *OC venture* for accessing the libraries, computational resources or support services. The *Computing Resource Providers* (a.k.a. nodes) are (i) connected with the OC Platform; (ii) responsible for providing infrastructural support, e.g., mining and/or consensus mechanisms, for the execution of smart contracts, and for providing the computational resources to support the OC functionality, and they receive some incentives for these services

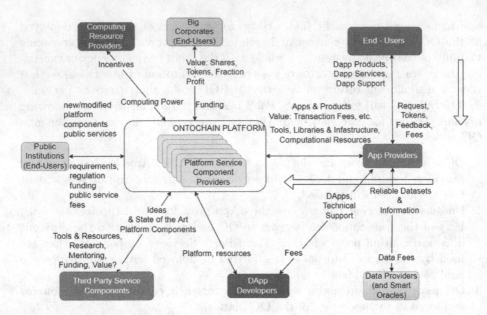

Fig. 2. The value network of OC.

(i.e., gas fees) in return from the OC platform. The *Data Providers* (i) provide data to *dApp providers* (and their smart contracts); (ii) might be smart oracles that provide trustworthy data or they may feed smart oracle data providers that are exterior to the OC platform or interior; (iii) get paid for the data that they provide by the end-users of dApps (directly or indirectly through *dApp providers*). Different cascades or hierarchies of data stores can be envisioned here as *Data Providers*. The *End-users* pay the *dApp providers* for the use of distributed applications. Note that *End Users* can be further distinguished in: 1) end user of a service provided by a company or a public institution; 2) end user of a P2P trading application. In the first case, end-users can pay directly or their fees to be subsidized by the company or by the public institution. Also, in trading applications (for goods or data), we may have to distinguish between sellers and buyers, although all have to pay, in cases where it makes sense that different amounts are charged to different end-user roles. *Corporate customers* or public administration customers also belong to this role and they may provide requirements and receive special services (e.g., BaaS, PaaS, SaaS, etc.) from the OC platform. The *Public Institutions* provide requirements/regulation to the OC platform. They may pay OC venture for utility services offered by the platform. The *Investors* may provide funding to OC in exchange of equities (or tokens of some form issued by the OC venture).

Table 1. (a) General economic parameters and (b) revenue parameters.

Economic Parameter	Value	Revenue Parameter	Value
Inflation rate	2%	Mean fee per dApp transaction	8 €
Interest loan rate	5%	Avg monthly dApp transactions per user	5
Credit period	5 years	Monthly fee per user per dApp	40€
Amortization period	5 years	dApp monthly OC hosting fee	100€
Electricity price	0.2 €/KWh	dApp deployment cost	100€
(a)		(b)	

7 Economic Analysis

7.1 The Economic Model

We will study this business plan concurrently for the main stakeholders involved in the described value network. Global assumptions and parameters of the ONTOCHAIN (OC) ecosystem are depicted in Table 1a. We assume the lifetime of the investment is 20 years. (Note that Bitcoin is 13 years old now and it is not going anywhere soon.) The start year of the investment is 2023 and the first operational year is 2024. In compliance to the common approach for economic analysis, we assume annual general expenses equal to the 8% of the annual revenues. For realistically assessing the economic viability of the OC platform, we consider that the initial capital investment is 6 M €, which is the total OC project funding. For revenue, CAPEX and OPEX parameters of the economic analysis, we performed a market analysis regarding the average transaction fee in Ethereum[4], the Neo system and network fees[5], the real costs running a dApp at EOS blockchain[6], the dApp hosting fees[7], the blockchain dApp development costs[8] and more. The revenue parameters are described in Table 1b. The OC platform is assumed to withhold 35% of the dApp service fees paid by the end-users. We assume that each dApp employs 4 OC Service Components on the average; each of these service components is paid a fraction 12% of the service fee per dApp transaction withheld by the OC platform.

All CAPEX parameters are depicted in Table 2, while OPEX parameters are depicted in Table 3. The CAPEX for the OC venture concern platform development and infrastructure costs (in terms of full nodes) as specified above. OC blockchain network is assumed initially to have 10 full nodes (e.g., i9 8-core 3GHz, 16GB RAM, 1TB SSD). The initial number of mining nodes is assumed to be 3. We assume a hardware expansion rate of 0.01% with respect to the number of monthly dapp transactions to be processed (i.e., 1 node per 10000

---

[4] https://ycharts.com/indicators/ethereum_average_transaction_fee.
[5] https://neo.org/.
[6] https://www.linkedin.com/pulse/real-cost-running-dApp-eos-network-h%C3%A9lder-vasconcelos/?articleId=6643471577910431744.
[7] https://ycharts.com/indicators/ethereum_average_transaction_fee.
[8] https://oyelabs.com/blockchain-app-development-cost/.

Table 2. The CAPEX parameters.

CAPEX Parameter	Value
dApp software development	50K €
HW cost per (mining) node (500MH/s)	7.5K €
HW cost per full OC node	3K €
Hardware cost per service component	5K €
Initial number of full OC nodes	5
EC funding for OC	6M €
dApp deployment cost (0.3 ETH)	600 €
Service Component SW Development	80K €

Table 3. OPEX parameters

OPEX Parameter	Value
Annual cost for SW licenses for OC	1000 €
Monthly power per mining node	1116 KWh
Gas fees per dApp transaction	2 €
Monthly rent for placing OC/SC node	10 €
dApp hosting fee per month	100 €
Annual personnel Costs for SW Maintenance, Marketing and Support (per dApp)	12K €
Monthly communication (network) costs per OC/SC node	40 €
Monthly computation power consumption per OC/SC node	720 KWh
Annual Personnel Costs for SW Maintenance, Marketing and Support (per Service Component)	48K €
Annual Personnel Costs for SW Maintenance, Marketing and Support (per dApp provider)	48K €
Communication (network) costs per service component/dApp provider	600 €
Annual OC personnel Costs for Software Maintenance, Marketing and Support (per dApp)	120 €
Monthly rent for placing a mining node	150 €
Monthly maintenance cost per mining node	200 €
Data fees	0.5 €/transaction

monthly transactions) both for the full and for the mining nodes. The OPEX for OC concern power costs, gas fees to validation nodes, rent or other hosting fees for OC full nodes, the OC personnel costs for software maintenance, marketing and support (per dApp), the software licensing and related costs and the networking costs. For the time being, we assume that gas fees of 2 € per dApp transaction are shared among the total number of mining nodes. Regarding software licenses, the OC platform is supposed to be paying 1,000 € for various licenses annually.

The CAPEX for an OC Service Component concern software development and hardware costs for supporting the functionality of the service component, i.e., servers, networking equipment, etc. The OPEX for an OC Service Component comprises hardware expansion with respect to the number of service requests as explained above, fees for the physical placement of the hardware (per service component node), annual personnel costs for software maintenance, marketing and support, power costs and networking cost.

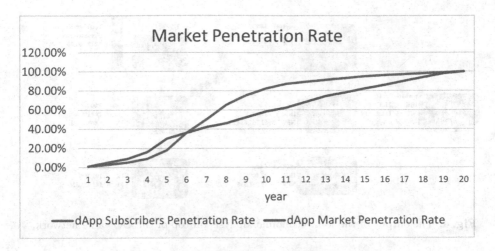

Fig. 3. Market penetration scenario.

The CAPEX for a dApp provider concern dApp software development and one-off cost for dApp deployment at the OC platform. Concerning the OPEX costs for a dApp provider these comprise the dApp hosting fee paid to the OC platform, the annual personnel cost for software maintenance and support, and the annual marketing costs (i.e., 10K €).

The CAPEX for a dApp developer concern hardware costs for a software-development PC (i.e., 5000 €). Its OPEX comprise software licences (i.e., 300 € annually), networking cost (i.e., 600 € annually) and electricity power costs (i.e., assuming 720KWh monthly electricity consumption).

The CAPEX for a data provider involves the cost for a high-end PC (i.e., 5,000 €). Depending on whether it also encapsulates the functionality of a smart oracle or not, it may also involve the development cost of a smart oracle functionality (i.e., 80,000 € as in the case of any service component). The OPEX for a data provider comprise software licenses and related costs (i.e., 1,000 €) when smart-oracle functionality is included, networking cost (i.e., 600 € annually), electricity power costs (i.e., 720 KWh monthly consumption per node at 0.2 €/KWh), and hardware scaling of 0.01% with respect to the number of transactions (as per service component). Moreover, the data provider is assumed to pay 20% of the data fees for acquiring the raw data.

Finally, the CAPEX for a mining node concern acquiring mining equipment, while the OPEX concern electricity power cost, network connectivity cost, a monthly maintenance fee and a monthly rent for hosting such a node.

7.2 Results

In this subsection, given the economic modeling of the OC ecosystem provided previously, we perform economic assessment of the sustainability of the OC ecosystem as a whole and for each stakeholder separately. The market penetration rate for the OC platform is considered as shown in Fig. 3. More specifically,

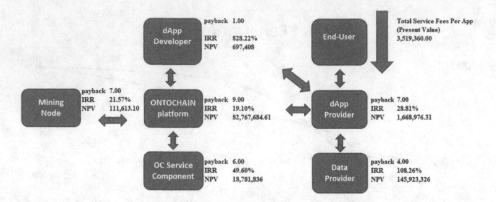

Fig. 4. The output of the joint economic analysis on top of the OC value network.

the number of dApp deployed at the platform increases quasi-linearly, while the number of end-users per dApp increases in a sigmoid manner. Overall, this is considered to be a moderate market penetration scenario.

We found the payback period, the internal rate of return (IRR) and the net present value (NPV) after 20 years for all stakeholders, as illustrated in Fig. 4. Observe that the OC ecosystem turned out to be profitable for all stakeholders, although not in a similar manner. Specifically, the OC venture is found to have an NPV of 82.7M €, a long payback period of 9 years and an impressive IRR of 19.1%. Considering that a 6M € initial investment was assumed for the OC venture, this result is quite acceptable in economic terms. Moreover, the NPV for an OC Service Component was found to be 18.78M €, with a remarkable IRR of 49.6% and a payback period of 6 years. Also, for a dApp provider we found a payback period of 7 years (with IRR 28.81%) and an NPV of 1.6 million €. A Data Provider was found to have a payback period of 4 years, an amazing IRR of 108.26% and an NPV of roughly 146M €. This result hints us that probably the raw data fees have been assumed to be too low. The dApp developer has a modest NPV of 700K €, but minimal capital investments are required with very short payback period of only 1 year. Roughly, the dApp developer is assumed to receive a salary of 50K € annually, which is an assumption to reconsider. The mining node was found to have a payback period of 7 years, an IRR of 21.5% and an NPN of 111.6K €. This economic output is clearly poor for a mining node. However, we assumed that 350 € are paid monthly for hosting and outsourcing the maintenance of the mining hardware, thus significantly reducing mining profits. Note that this is not typical as, such a small mining infrastructure, is normally hosted at the premises of a tech savvy individual that enrolls personally into maintenance. All the value is inserted into the OC ecosystem by the end-users of dApps; total service fees paid per dApp in a 20-years horizon is assumed to be 3.5 million €.

The annual net cash flow and the EBITDA for the OC venture are depicted in Fig. 5a and Fig. 5b. Observe the negative flows in the first years until the break

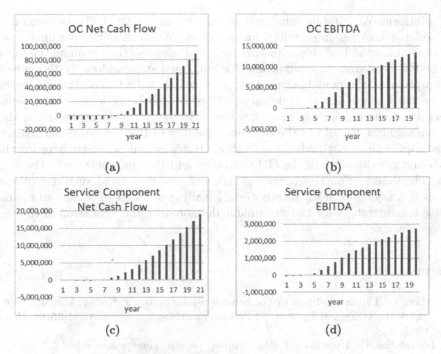

Fig. 5. (a) Net cash flow and (b) EBITDA for OC (a),(b) respectively and for Service Component (c),(d) respectively.

even point on the 9th year. The annual net cash flow and the EBITDA for a OC Service Component are depicted in Fig. 5c and Fig. 5d. Observe the almost zero profit in the first 7 years, and the minimal negative flows that could be serviced by a low loan.

However, building a win-win outcome for the stakeholders of the OC ecosystem cannot be taken for granted. For example, let us assume that OC service components each demand 20% (instead of 12%) from the dApp service fees withheld by the OC platform per dApp transaction. Then, the payback period for the OC becomes prohibitively high (i.e., 17 years!), while the IRR becomes only 3.34%, which makes the OC venture not worth pursuing. At the same time, the payback period for an OC service component still remains 6 years, while IRR was already very high. Thus, a small modification in the revenue sharing scheme made the ecosystem economically unviable.

8   Conclusion

Multi-tier jointly-developed decentralized ecosystems are hard to transform to business and operate as a sustainable economy, due to conflicting incentives and lack of coordination. We considered the case of the ONTOCHAIN (OC) software ecosystem, where a venture takes over, manages and maintains the jointly-built

OC platform. We carefully analyzed all stakeholders in the OC ecosystem and defined the business interactions among them. We defined the parameters of an economic model of this value network and assessed the economic viability of the OC ecosystem as a whole and for individual stakeholders. With realistic assumptions in the model parameters, we found that the OC ecosystem can be a *win-win* business for all stakeholders involved and bring high value to end-users at an affordable cost. Finally, we established that revenue sharing in this system significantly affects the economic viability of the different stakeholders. This implies that maximalistic individual strategies can be destructive for the economic sustainability of the OC ecosystem and thus unprofitable in the long run. The design of an appropriate governance model to avoid such destructive forces is a key concern for future work. Finally, we intend to design an appropriate token strategy for the sustainable development and expansion of the OC ecosystem.

References

1. Allee, V.: The art and practice of being a revolutionary. J. Knowl. Manag. (1999)
2. Curtis, B., Kellner, M.I., Over, J.: Process modeling. Commun. ACM **35**(9), 75–90 (1992)
3. Foundation H: Hyperledger fabric: open, proven, enterprise-grade DLT (2020). https://www.hyperledger.org/wp-content/uploads/2020/03/hyperledger_fabric_whitepaper.pdf
4. Morkunas, V.J., Paschen, J., Boon, E.: How blockchain technologies impact your business model. Bus. Horiz. **62**(3), 295–306 (2019)
5. Mukhopadhyay, S., Bouwman, H.: Multi-actor collaboration in platform-based ecosystem: opportunities and challenges. J. Inf. Technol. Case Appl. Res. **20**(2), 47–54 (2018)
6. Nakamoto, S.: Bitcoin: a peer-to-peer electronic cash system. Decentralized Business Review, p. 21260 (2008)
7. Osterwalder, A., Pigneur, Y.: Business Model Generation: A Handbook for Visionaries, Game Changers, and Challengers, vol. 1. Wiley, Hoboken (2010)
8. Papaioannou, T.G., et al.: A new blockchain ecosystem for trusted, traceable and transparent ontological knowledge management. In: Tserpes, K., et al. (eds.) GECON 2021. LNCS, vol. 13072, pp. 93–105. Springer, Cham (2021). https://doi.org/10.1007/978-3-030-92916-9_8
9. Porter, M.E., Advantage, C.: Creating and sustaining superior performance. Competitive Advantage **167**, 167–206 (1985)
10. Wood, G., et al.: Ethereum: a secure decentralised generalised transaction ledger. Ethereum Project Yellow Paper **151**(2014), 1–32 (2014)

HOCC: An Ontology for Holistic Description of Cluster Settings

Yannis Poulakis[1,2]([✉]) [iD], Georgios Fatouros[1,3] [iD], George Kousiouris[4],
and Dimosthenis Kyriazis[1] [iD]

[1] University of Piraeus, Piraeus, Greece
{gpoul,dimos}@unipi.gr
[2] Byte Computer, Athens, Greece
[3] Innov-Acts Ltd., Nicosia, Cyprus
gfatouros@innov-acts.com
[4] Harokopio University, Athens, Greece
gkousiou@hua.gr

Abstract. Ontologies have become the de-facto information representation method in the semantic web domain, but recently gained popularity in other domains such as cloud computing. In this context, ontologies enable service discovery, effective comparison and selection of IaaS, PaaS and SaaS offerings and ease the application deployment process by tackling what is known as the vendor lock-in problem. In this paper we propose a novel ontology named HOCC: holistic ontology for effective cluster comparison. The ontology design process is based on four different information categories, namely Performance, SLA, cost and environmental impact. In addition we present our approach for populating, managing and taking advantage of the proposed ontology as developed in a real world Kubernetes cluster setting, as well as instantiating the ontology with example services and data (namely performance aspects of a serverless function).

Keywords: ontology · cloud-computing · semantic-web · Kubernetes · OWL

1 Introduction

The amount of processing power that modern applications require, calls for infrastructures that can handle the workload that is generated, efficiently, in a fault tolerant manner and with respect to their environmental footprint [14]. To that end the cloud and edge computing paradigms have emerged, providing the necessary solutions for resource and service provisioning. Edge specifically, additionally provides the necessary tools to bring processing and storage close to the data sources while also adding resource mobility and low energy consumption

The research leading to the results presented in this paper has received funding from the European Union's funded Project PHYSICS under grant agreement no 101017047.

J. Á. Bañares et al. (Eds.): GECON 2022, LNCS 13430, pp. 41–49, 2023.
https://doi.org/10.1007/978-3-031-29315-3_4

[8]. Usually such clusters are formed via the use of Kubernetes [15], an open-source cluster management software that also provides alternative distributions for edge clusters [16].

The plethora of available cluster composition schemata, calls for distinction of the accompanying advantages and disadvantages of each one. This holds especially true in multi-cluster scenarios, where several clusters are managed by a central hub and the options for application or service deployment vary. To tackle this problem, we propose a formal cluster description schema that is based on Web Ontology Language (OWL) [4] and a system that enables automated retrieval of information from Kubernetes-based clusters, transformation according to the ontology definitions into named individuals and storage into a graph database. In essence the main contributions of this paper can be summarized as follows:

- Design of a novel ontology that is based on four different pillars of information (Performance and Technical Properties, SLA Description, Cost Evaluation, Environmental Impact), necessary for a holistic approach in cluster comparison.
- An architecture that enables population, management and information retrieval of the proposed ontology tested against a real world Kubernetes cluster.

In Sect. 2 we present related works in ontologies for cloud computing. Section 3 analyses our ontology design rationale and Sect. 4 demonstrates the ontology population method, evaluation and an example of instantiation. Finally Sects. 5 concludes our work while also presenting our future work directions.

2   Related Work

One of the earlier works in ontologies that focuses on depicting information on cloud resources was that of moSAIC [12] in which authors utilize ontologies to describe functional and non functional aspects of cloud computing to tackle service negotiation between provider and consumer. In a similar fashion authors of [17] use an OWL-based ontology to address several features and concepts that are directly connected to the cloud computing paradigm while also displaying how this ontology is populated on an Azure Kubernetes cluster through SPARQL queries. CL-Ontology [6] extends mOSAIC by incorporating additional semantics to support interoperability of HPC environments in the cloud.

Service Level Agreement (SLA) document description through a common vocabulary, has also gained attention in the semantics domain. The EU horizon project SLALOM contributed to a formal description of SLA characteristics extending from the 19086-2 standard of the International Organization for Standardization (ISO). In [3] the authors propose an ontology schema that is appropriate for depicting SLA terms and their various properties and relationships and a method of automatic information extraction through SLA public documents via pattern matching.

In [13] and [2] the authors utilize the ontology paradigm to assess the service discovery in the cloud via semantic cloud service representation. In the latter authors also display experimental results when compared to google searches of three different specified queries. In a similar fashion in [10] authors propose an ontology based system that allows for effective queries when searching the necessary cloud resources for the deployment of a user specified job.

The work of Borisova et al. [5] displays several examples on how the TOSCA ontology modelling schema can be adapted to describe a variety of Kubernetes specifics. Focusing on the PaaS offerings specifically, authors of [3] define a PaaS marketplace that is based on the ontology information representation schema.

Authors of [9] present challenges that are presented when modelling cloud services with ontologies as emerged from the practical application of the UFO-S ontology. Finally the recent work [1] presents some of current works in the field and addresses new opportunities that arise with the use of ontologies in cloud computing.

3 Ontology Design

Ontologies in computer science, provide a structural format in order to represent information about certain entities and their respective properties and relationships mainly through classes, subclasses, object and data properties. In the presented ontology we consider the class *:Cluster* and *:ClusterNode* direct subclasses of *owl:thing* to be cornerstone entities of this ontology. Throughout this section, we use the blank ":" to state terms that are defined in the designed ontology. For a more thorough examination of all entities we suggest visualization of the ontology as uploaded in our github repository[1].

We expect the produced ontology to be populated and utilized in order to compare and therefore select clusters for application deployment in a holistic manner. This realization is the base of our design process and leads us to the distinction of four different pylons that encapsulate necessary aspects for cluster description. Namely these aspects are the following: *(a) Performance and Technical Properties (b) SLA Description, (c) Cost Evaluation, (d) Environmental Impact*. All of the ontology formulation process has been realized with the use of the graphical tool Protégé, a staple in ontology modelling.

3.1 Performance and Technical Properties

First we consider in the ontology design different resource characteristics that will eventually match certain requirements that are derived from the application modelling process. These characteristics display hardware information (GPU enabled nodes, Ram and CPU capabilities, etc.), software information (OS image, Hypervisor, etc.) and generic properties (Location, IP, etc.)

---

[1] https://github.com/yannispoulakis/HOCC/blob/main/HOCC-Ontology.owl.

Typically a cluster's computational capabilities derive from node aspects, thus we couple the *:ClusterNode* class with the appropriate properties. Specifically, nodes are connected with *:VirtualUnit* or *:PhysicalUnit* via the *:isHostedOn* property. The physical unit class aims to cover bare metal nodes in the form of edge nodes or on premises bare-metal computers, while the virtual unit can refer to both private or provided by cloud vendors virtual machines. In addition, the "unit" couple of classes are connected to the *:RawComputationalResource* class which consists the *:Ram,* *:GPU* and *:CPU* subclasses that include the necessary properties for defining the allocatable respective values. We create a series of object and data properties that link the classes among them and with real values describing their capabilities. In addition we incorporate the *:benchmark* class that aims to describe certain workloads that tested against a cluster to provide a performance indication.

3.2   SLA

One additional aspect we consider in the design process is the depiction of information that is found in service level agreements (SLA), such as the terms and conditions to be met cloud providers as stated in the respective public documents of the services they refer to. Differences in how the cloud providers describe similar SLA terms leads to inconsistencies on how services are compared, monitored and in turn selected for a given task. In the presented ontology we select to describe SLA terms as different classes with a group of properties that depict their respective information. This includes the definition of metrics, their target value and the respective rebate in case of agreement breach.

More specifically we define the parent class *:ServiceLevelAgreement*, bind to *:CloudService*, that is related with terms via the *:hasSLATerm* to the presented terms. Each *:ServiceLevelAgreementTerm* comes with a set of data properties that define target values, type of measurement and definition as presented in Fig. 1.

3.3   Cost

A clear overview of cluster expenses that come with setup, maintenance and scaling is a key factor to enable cost optimization. For private and hybrid clouds that utilize bare metal machines as nodes and certain software units, such as specific OS or hypervisors, we think as appropriate to capture the cost per acquisition of both software and hardware necessary for the cluster realization. For clusters that are based fully or partially on cloud provider offerings we declare a set of classes that capture the various pricing models. To that end we define the *physics:CostSchema* class which consists of four different subclasses that represent the basis of different cost schemata. Table 1 gives a formal overview of the defined specialized classes. The parent class *physics:CostSchema* is also assigned certain properties that define the currency used to measure pricing model, namely *physics:withCurrencyValue* and *physics:withCurrencyType* that are inherited to all subclasses and are of type *rdf:string* and *rdfs:decimal* respectively.

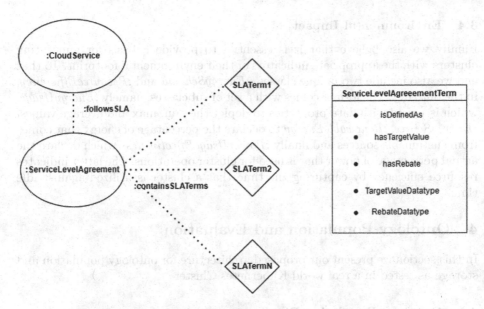

Fig. 1. Ontology formation of the SlA classes and their accompanying data properties.

Table 1. Subclasses of the specialized CostSchema parent class.

Subclasses	Usage
:CostPerAcquisition	*Acquisition cost of hardware and software units.*
:CostPerRequest	*Cost per request. Used in cases such as storage and serverless.*
:CostPerTimePeriod	*Pricing per units of time. Most commonly measured by hour or seconds.*
:CostPerSpecialUnit	*Special case for defining custom units of pricing measurements.*

We consider the case of serverless function offering pricing model, as described in the Lambda service of AWS, as a use case to validate our modelling approach. This type of service, combines charges per request and execution time, thus we opt to allow classes of Table 1 to exist jointly. Furthermore the execution time rates vary depending on the amount of memory and ephemeral storage configured for the function to be executed. To that end we assign four different data properties to the *:CostSchema* class, *:withFactor*, *:withFactorValue*, *:CostAlterationOperation* and *:CostAlterationValue*. Additionally both of these charging factors take place after a certain threshold has been exceeded thus we define the data properties *:overThreshold* and *:underThreshold* to define certain lower and upper limits of the respective measurement unit that start the charging process.

3.4   Environmental Impact

Finally we also believe that it is essential to provide a basis for annotating clusters with the appropriate indicators of their environmental footprint. To that end we also include two unique classes, *:EnergySchema* and *:ResourceEfficiency*, in the ontology. The former comes with a set of subclasses, namely *:EnergyUsage*, which is paired with data properties to depict the min, max and average values, *:EnergySource*, *:RenewableEnergy* to declare the percentage of energy that comes from sustainable sources and finally *:PowerUsageEffectiveness* which declare the actual percentage of power that is used for cluster operations. The latter indicates resource efficiency by capturing the time that a cluster is utilized against idle time.

4   Ontology Population and Evaluation

In this section we present our proposed architecture for ontology population and storage as tested in a real world Kubernetes Cluster.

4.1   Ontology Population Pipeline

Figure 2 presents an overview of our proposed architecture, for ontology population from kubernetes clusters. We opt to base our development for compatibility with the Kubernetes ecosystem, due to its widespread adoption, community support and efficiency. A developed pod, which is the Kubernetes unit of deployment, is deployed in each of the available clusters that we aim to extract information from. Afterwards each pod loads the respective cluster configuration through the Kubernetes python client and makes calls to the Kubernetes API to extract the available raw information. Deployment of this pod also includes a set of coupled permissions that are declared according to the Kubernetes Role-based access control (RBAC) method.

Afterwards, with the use of OWLReady2[2] we process the output of the Kubernetes API calls and define the produced individuals along with their properties, while following the guidelines of the proposed ontology. In certain cases this procedure is straight forward such as checking the computational aspects of a node via the list-nodes command. In other cases we perform a keyword search to implicitly identify information. Finally we serialize this kind of information in the Turtle syntax so it can be stored and further used by semantic reasoners. To accommodate for information that cannot be accessed via the Kubernetes API, we also include in our code a graphical interface for manual creation of individuals.

All of our code is available in our GitHub project repository[3]. It contains both the ontology in a raw XML format and the individuals creation methods wrapped in a python flask service. Additionally the project repository contains the necessary files for docker image creation and cluster deployment.

---

[2] https://readthedocs.org/projects/owlready2/downloads/pdf/latest/.
[3] https://github.com/yannispoulakis/HOCC.

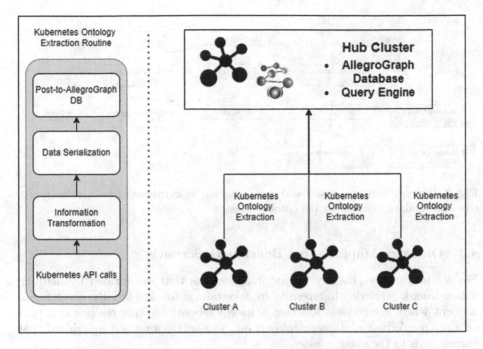

Fig. 2. Proposed pipeline for extracting and managing Kubernetes cluster specific information according to the ontology design.

4.2   Ontology Evaluation

In this section we present two different ontology evaluation measures that have been previously used in the literature [7,11], namely Relationships Richness (RR) and Attributes Richness (AR). Formally, these metrics are calculated by Eqs. 1 and 2. The Relationships Richness metric reflects the diversity of relationships and is the ratio of existing relationships in the ontology divided by the number of subclasses and relationships. We report this value to be 0.4 for our ontology. Additionally the Attributes richness defines how many data properties on average classes have tied to. It is the ratio of all data properties divided by the number of classes and the respective value for our ontology is 0.6578, which is slightly higher than other IT related ontologies (0.65 in [7]). The comparison of the RR indicates a lower value in our case (0.4 compared to 0.55), owed to the fact that the four different categories of consideration (energy, cost, performance and SLA) need to be mapped primarily as subclasses. Unfortunately metrics for the most similar ontologies defined in Sect. 2 were not available from the respective publications.

$$PR = \frac{|P|}{|SC| + |P|} \tag{1}$$

$$AR = \frac{|ATT|}{|C|} \tag{2}$$

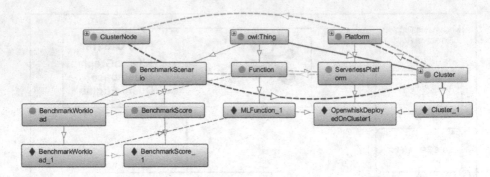

Fig. 3. Example benchmark scenario representation by individuals forming the respective relationships asserted by the ontology design.

4.3   Ontology Mapping to a Benchmark Scenario

Finally in Fig. 3 we display the interconnections that are formed by defining a benchmark scenario that results to a certain score. Essentially we define a concept where a serverless function is used for benchmarking reasons and runs on the OpenWhisk platform deployed on "Cluster1", a named individual that corresponds to the class *:cluster*.

5   Conclusions and Future Work

Throughout this work we have presented a novel ontology design for the characterization of cloud computing services and clusters based on four different information categories. We have also showcased our approach for populating the ontology in a real-world scenario that considers Kubernetes formed clusters. We believe the usage of ontologies in cloud and edge computing for multi dimensional characterization of clusters will play a critical role in selecting services and cloud resources in a holistic manner. Future work may include optimizations and extraction methods that may provide further information on cluster hardware, as well as specific software or configuration abilities of a given cluster. These may include for example specific policies followed by the cluster owner, like scheduling or priority capabilities.

References

1. Agbaegbu, J., Arogundade, O.T., Misra, S., Damaševičius, R.: Ontologies in cloud computing-review and future directions. Future Internet **13**(12), 302 (2021)
2. Ali, A., Shamsuddin, S.M., Eassa, F.E.: Ontology-based cloud services representation. Res. J. Appl. Sci. Eng. Technol. **8**(1), 83–94 (2014)
3. Bassiliades, N., Symeonidis, M., Gouvas, P., Kontopoulos, E., Meditskos, G., Vlahavas, I.P.: Paasport semantic model: an ontology for a platform-as-a-service semantically interoperable marketplace. Data Knowl. Eng. **113**, 81–115 (2018)

4. Bechhofer, S., et al.: OWL web ontology language reference. W3C Recommendation **10**(2), 1–53 (2004)
5. Borisova, A., Shvetcova, V., Borisenko, O.: Adaptation of the TOSCA standard model for the Kubernetes container environment. In: 2020 Ivannikov Memorial Workshop (IVMEM), pp. 9–14. IEEE (2020)
6. Castañé, G.G., Xiong, H., Dong, D., Morrison, J.P.: An ontology for heterogeneous resources management interoperability and HPC in the cloud. Futur. Gener. Comput. Syst. **88**, 373–384 (2018)
7. Hasan, M.M., Kousiouris, G., Anagnostopoulos, D., Stamati, T., Loucopoulos, P., Nikolaidou, M.: CISMET: a semantic ontology framework for regulatory-requirements-compliant information systems development and its application in the GDPR case. Int. J. Semant. Web Inf. Syst. (IJSWIS) **17**(1), 1–24 (2021)
8. Khan, W.Z., Ahmed, E., Hakak, S., Yaqoob, I., Ahmed, A.: Edge computing: a survey. Futur. Gener. Comput. Syst. **97**, 219–235 (2019)
9. Livieri, B., et al.: Ontology-based modeling of cloud services: challenges and perspectives. In: Proceedings of Short and Doctoral Consortium Papers Presented at the 8th IFIP WG 8.1 Working Conference on the Practice of Enterprise Modelling (PoEM 2015), Valencia, Spain, 10–12 November 2015, vol. 1497, pp. 61–70. RWTH (2015)
10. Ma, Y.B., Jang, S.H., Lee, J.S.: Ontology-based resource management for cloud computing. In: Nguyen, N.T., Kim, C.-G., Janiak, A. (eds.) ACIIDS 2011. LNCS (LNAI), vol. 6592, pp. 343–352. Springer, Heidelberg (2011). https://doi.org/10.1007/978-3-642-20042-7_35
11. Mazzola, L., Kapahnke, P., Vujic, M., Klusch, M.: CDM-core: a manufacturing domain ontology in OWL2 for production and maintenance. In: KEOD, pp. 136–143 (2016)
12. Moscato, F., Aversa, R., Di Martino, B., Fortiş, T.F., Munteanu, V.: An analysis of mosaic ontology for cloud resources annotation. In: 2011 Federated Conference on Computer Science and Information Systems (FedCSIS), pp. 973–980. IEEE (2011)
13. Rekik, M., Boukadi, K., Ben-Abdallah, H.: Cloud description ontology for service discovery and selection. In: 2015 10th International Joint Conference on Software Technologies (ICSOFT), vol. 1, pp. 1–11. IEEE (2015)
14. Siddik, M.A.B., Shehabi, A., Marston, L.: The environmental footprint of data centers in the united states. Environ. Res. Lett. **16**(6), 064017 (2021)
15. Thurgood, B., Lennon, R.G.: Cloud computing with Kubernetes cluster elastic scaling. In: Proceedings of the 3rd International Conference on Future Networks and Distributed Systems, pp. 1–7 (2019)
16. Xiong, Y., Sun, Y., Xing, L., Huang, Y.: Extend cloud to edge with Kubeedge. In: 2018 IEEE/ACM Symposium on Edge Computing (SEC), pp. 373–377. IEEE (2018)
17. Zhang, Q., Haller, A., Wang, Q.: CoCoOn: cloud computing ontology for IaaS price and performance comparison. In: Ghidini, C., et al. (eds.) ISWC 2019. LNCS, vol. 11779, pp. 325–341. Springer, Cham (2019). https://doi.org/10.1007/978-3-030-30796-7_21

Effect of Trust and Institutional Quality on Cloud Federation Formation Using Agent-Based Modeling

Yodit Gebrealif(iD) and Jörn Altmann(⊠) (iD)

Technology Management, Economics, and Policy Program, College of Engineering, Seoul National University, Seoul, South Korea
jorn.altmann@acm.org

Abstract. Cloud providers make decisions on whom to interact with based on trust between cloud service providers. However, achieving trust has been a major obstacle to a wide cloud federation adoption. It has been observed that trust is largely determined by the provider, but trust can also be influenced by the external environment (such as by institutional trust, cultural trust, or legal framework) as well as by government policies or strategies. As a result of the cloud federation model, participants from different countries can collaborate with each other, sharing resources, transferring data, and exchanging knowledge, which is directly influenced by an organizational trust as well as institutional trust. Transferring data from one jurisdiction to another requires a legal framework and is a sensitive issue. Data protection concerns are not adequately addressed in a similar way in all countries, which negatively impacts trust. In this paper, we discuss trust from the perspective of institutional trust and propose an evaluation mechanism for trust during cloud federation formation. The proposed trust evaluation model utilizes neighbors' feedback and institutional quality, to evaluate the cloud service provider trust. The evaluation of the model is conducted by utilizing an agent-based approach and the Netlogo simulation tool. The results show that the proposed model generates profit in the three scenarios while the comparative model, which doesn't consider institutional trust, generates profits in only the two scenarios.

Keywords: Trusted Cloud Federation · Institutional Quality · Trust · Regulatory Quality · Cloud Federation Formation · Cloud Coalition Formation · Agent-Based Modeling · Agent-Based Simulation · Cooperative Formation · Rule of Law

1 Introduction

Cloud computing brings a large number of services to customers with low infrastructure costs [1, 2]. Customers access these services, work online, and store their data in the cloud [3]. Data is stored in the cloud without the customers knowing where the data is located and relocated, who has the access to the data, or from where the data is accessed [4]. As a consequence, data privacy, protection, and confidentiality have become the

J. Á. Bañares et al. (Eds.): GECON 2022, LNCS 13430, pp. 50–61, 2023.
https://doi.org/10.1007/978-3-031-29315-3_5

major issue in cloud computing. Especially in the data economy era, data is the future economic power of the government and enterprises. Consequently, the government and cloud service providers (CSP) need to assure that the citizen's (clients') data is protected and safe [5, 6]. The data safety issue is even more challenging when it comes to cloud federation (CF), which allows CSP to rent the resources from another provider when the demand exceeds the supply, and to rent out whenever other providers need to share their loads [7–10]. During this process, the customer data can be located or relocated to different countries with an agreement between the CSPs but without a cloud customer's consent. It affects the trust between the CSP and cloud customers [6] (Fig. 1).

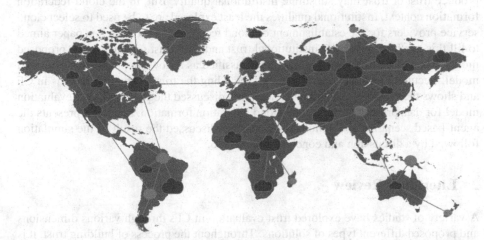

Fig. 1. Logical representation of CSPs integration.

Trust establishment and evaluation across CSPs have been defined as a prerequisite and critical requirement for participation in a CF, to utilize computing resources effectively [8, 11, 12]. Trust in cloud federation refers to the home cloud perception regarding the foreign cloud behaviors, which influences the decision of the home cloud to choose the foreign cloud and establish a CF [7, 13, 14]. It is a factor that has long been seen as a measure of evaluation, which serves as a foundation for decision-making regarding the extent to which the entity would behave as predicted. This measure of assessment needs some input to be calculated. In this research, those inputs are called factors (determinants) and are explored. Apart from these determinants, trust has been an issue in cloud federation [8, 15], and it can be seen in three dimensions: trust between client and CSP, between a CSP and other CSPs, and between a CSP and a CF. This study focuses on the trust evaluation during the partner selection process for establishing a CF considering customers' data safety and privacy.

Data protection and privacy are other important factors apart from trust, to be considered in a cloud federation formation. Since various cloud providers own data centers located in different geographical locations, it allows the provider to offer services to their target audience in a particular region. Therefore, data location and relocation in CF is the main concern, especially for a country with data location restriction. Moreover, studies from international trade [16] and the strategic alliance domain [17] justify that partners' trust and institutional quality (IQ) are mutually inclusive. The favorable impact of trust on commerce is conditional on IQ. Similarly, establishing a CF should favor the partner CSP's trustworthiness and the country's data protection capability. In existing cloud federation formation (CFF) strategies [4, 7–15], various types of trust sources, including SLA [27, 28], reputation [24, 27, 29] recommendation [26], feedback from users [17, 19], and from another cloud providers [18], are utilized as a trusted source to measure the CSP's trustworthiness. However, the formal institution quality along with the cloud providers' trust hasn't been well-explored as a parameter for partner selection.

In a study from International trade [16], it is justified that institution quality may produce trust or trust may substitute institutional quality. But, in the cloud federation formation context, Institutional qualities the least explored are to be used to select cloud service providers for the establishment of cloud federation. Therefore this paper aimed to fill this gap by considering institutional trust and CSP trust together in the proposed model. Therefore, the following section is classified as follows to present the proposed model. Section 2 presents related reviews regarding the trust evaluation models in CF and shows the previous research gap. Section 3 discussed the proposed trust evaluation model for data protection during the cloud federation formation. Section 4 presents the agent-based scenarios and simulation. Section 5 discussed the result of the simulation followed by a discussion and conclusion in Sect. 6.

2 Literature Review

A variety of studies have explored trust evaluation in CFs through various dimensions and proposed different types of solutions. Throughout the process of building trust, it is continuously updated in different stages. Moreover, the trust evaluation output of one stage will be the input for the next stage, and it continues in a round way that does not stop at a certain stage. Similarly, trust can be established in CFs through various CF stages, from partner selection until the end of the CF lifecycle. Through the procedure, determinants are used as input to the trust evaluation model to measure the trust level. A significant determinant used to evaluate the CSP trust level during the partner selection phase was explored in extensive studies. Muhammad et al. [18] have proposed a trust evaluation model that helps cloud service clients to identify and select trustworthy CSPs. In the proposed evaluation model, CSP data from regulatory bodies, about CSP performance, and feedback from users were used as a trusted source, to identify the trusted CSPs. Ghafoorian et al. [30] proposed a direct and indirect trust evaluation model. The authors have addressed the reputation-based role-based access control and the accuracy requirements for the indirect trust model for storing the data storage cloud settings safely. Similarly, several determinants are used in research to be able to measure the CSP's trustworthiness. The prior widely used trust determinant is a previous experience [20, 23, 31]. The previous interactions incorporate the number of SLA violations [20, 32], previous successful transactions [31], or the probability prediction of mistrust cost for different SLA parameters proposed by a CSP [23]. They are used as trust metrics for determining whether to cooperate again or interact with a new partner. Moreover, Naseer et al. [18] present a trust model that utilizes various parameters including downtime, uptime, SLA parameters, security measures, and data from regulatory bodies. The one-year transaction data accumulates in the regulatory bodies and this data is utilized to see the history of the CSP's success.

Furthermore, recommendations [12, 13], reputations [12, 14], or feedback [14–16] have been utilized in different studies as a determinant to evaluate trust with/without previous interaction parameters. Dhole et al. [12] present that previous interactions of CSP and recommendations are utilized to be able to learn about the CSP and to recommend it to another participant that does not have previous interactions. Moreover, Ahmed et al. [33] present the recommendation and feedback-based trust evaluation to establish CF. It deals with excluding false feedback and recommendations by taking previous successful transactional history into consideration. Lastly, few studies use determinants like recommendation, feedback, and reputation in addition to successful interactions. As an example, Mashayekhy et al. [20] propose a cloud federation formation mechanism utilizing previous interaction information, if it exists, or reputation, if the interaction history does not exist.

Overall, the literature review depicts that different determinants have been used as input to the trust evaluation model. It is clear that all these determinants address different dimensions to evaluate trust. However, the literature analysis also shows that trust regarding data protection is the least explored research area. Especially, the institution's trust level, along with the CSP trust, has not been examined, detailing where the data is physically located, the availability of data protection policy, and the government's effectiveness. Therefore, this paper aimed to fill the gap in trust in data protection by considering the governance indicators as an additional parameter along with feedback and reputation-based CSP trust.

3   Proposed Trust Evaluation Model

CF can be established within a country or across countries, considering different parameters [34, 35]. Trust is one of the main parameters to be evaluated among these parameters. A trust evaluation model is proposed for selecting trusted partners during the process of building cross-border CFs. CSP trust and institutional trust are represented by the overall trust (Global Trust). Therefore, this study divides global trust into two: *CSP Trust* and *Institutional Trust*. The CSP trust is an expectation about the candidate CSP that will react as expected. Institutional trust is the expectation of the country's rule of law, the readiness with regard to regulatory quality, data protection, related policy availability, and government effectiveness.

3.1   Model Description

Global Trust: As the effect of CSP trust in the presence of institutional trust with respect to data protection is the main objective of this study, global trust is calculated as the mean of the CSP trust and institutional trust (Eq. 1):

$$GlobalTrust_i = mean(CSPTrust_i + InstitutionalTrust_i) \tag{1}$$

Using this model, the trust of each provider is calculated. The results are used for selecting trusted CSPs and establishing CF.

CSP Trust: The trust of a CSP_i is computed based on the satisfaction level of peer CSPs that have experience with the CSP_i. Depending on the level of satisfaction, the peer CSPs express their opinion about the CSP_i. The feedback from each peer CSP_j is given a value between 1 and 5. 1 indicates the lowest feedback level, which indicates the peer CSP_j dissatisfaction with the previous interaction with CSP_i, and 5 indicates that the peer CSP_j is highly satisfied with the performance of the focal CSP_i:

$$AvgFeedback_i = \frac{\sum_{j=1}^{feedbackGiver_i} Feedback_{j \to i}}{feedbackGiver_i} \quad (2)$$

The average feedback value, which is in the range between 1 and 5, is normalized by employing the Eq. 3, defining and measuring the CSP trust. Therefore, the CSP trust is in the range between 0 and 1. A value of 0 means that the CSP is not trusted, while a value of 1 represents that the CSP is trusted according to the recommendations given by the peer CSPs.

$$CSPTrust_i = \frac{AvgFeedback_i - MinAvgFeedback_i}{MaxAvgFeedback_i - MinAvgFeedback_i} \quad (3)$$

where $MinAvgFeedback_i$ is the minimal feedback value 1, and $MaxAvgFeedback_i$ is the maximum feedback value 5.

Institutional Trust: Institutional trust is the other dimension addressed by the proposed model. It includes the country's rule of law, the readiness with regard to regulatory quality, data protection policy availability, and government effectiveness. Institutional trust is measured through various parameters, but, for the sake of simplicity, we utilize three parameters: namely data protection policy availability (PA) [36], data protection policy quality (QA) [37], and global or national cyber security index of the country (CI) where the CSP data center is located [38]. The variable PA measures the availability of data protection policy hence if the policy is available, the PA value will be 1 but if not the PA value will be 0. The QA is the quality of the available data protection policy and it is a subjective measure of the CSP depending on its policy preference. The last CI variable represents the national cyber security index with a value between 0 and 1. Depending on the weights given, the institutional trust of a trustee is calculated as shown in the following equation:

$$InstitutionalTrust_i^{Country} = \alpha_1 PA_i + \alpha_2 QA_i + \alpha_3 CI_i \quad Where \ \alpha_1 + \alpha_2 + \alpha_3 = 1 \quad (4)$$

3.2 Cloud Federation Formation

Evaluating the proposed trust model is performed by utilizing the following CFF algorithm. In the algorithm, the *requester CSP* refers to the CSP who initiates the interaction to establish CF and the *peer CSPs* refer to the requested CSP to join the CF. The process of establishing CF consists of 9 main steps.

1. Set initial parameters (PA_i, QA_i, CI_i, $Trust_{threshold}$, $Profit_i$)

2. CSP_i defines the value of α_1, α_2, α_3 and calculate Institutional Trust
3. CSP_i = get feedback ($Feedback_{j->i}$) from all peer CSP_j
4. Calculate the Global Trust $GlobalTrust_i = mean(CSPTrust_i + InstitutionalTrust_i)$
5. Can CSP_i find peers CSP_j randomly and doesn't have an existing link between them?

    a. If Yes go to step 6
    b. If No go to END

6. Is the peer CSP_j global trust $\geq Trust_{threshold}$

    a. If Yes go to step 7
    b. If No go to steps 5

7. Create the link between CSP_i and peer CSP_j to joining a cloud federation
8. Calculate the CSP_i profit $Profit_i := \frac{\sum_{j=1}^{n} Profit_j}{n}$ where n is the total number of CSPs in CF
9. Go to step 5

4 Simulation Model Scenario

The proposed model evaluation is performed by an agent-based modeling approach, utilizing the Netlogo simulation tool. In addition, the assumption is that the average feedback is collected by an external system (feedback collector system). Therefore, only the outcome of the feedback collector system is utilized in this model. Given the assumption, the following four scenarios are designed to evaluate the proposed model behavior.

Scenario 1 - High feedback with high institutional quality index: This scenario aims to represent the CSP_i located in the country with high institutional trust in terms of data protection policy, cyber security, and data protection quality along with a good reputation in the neighbor's peer providers CSP_j. This CSP_i delivers a good service and gains a high level of feedback-based reputation.

Scenario 2 - High feedback with low institutional quality index: This scenario represents the CSP_i with high feedback but located in a country that has no or low institutional trust. CSP_i obtains good feedback from peers CSP_j by providing trusted services to these CSPs. However, the country's level of trust in terms of data protection is low due to the quality of the policy or the low level of national cyber security of the country.

Scenario 3 - Low feedback with high institutional quality index: In this scenario, the CSP is located in a country with a high-quality data protection policy but the feedback-based reputation of CSP_i stated by the neighbor CSP_j is low. On the one hand, this scenario can represent new entrant small-scale CSPs located in high-institutional-quality countries. But due to high market competition with the current giant providers in the market, the CSPs face difficulties in earning high reputations. On the other hand, this

Table 1. Simulation Setup and Configuration.

Variable	Scenario-1	Scenario-2	Scenario-3	Scenario-4
$feedbackGiver_i$	100	100	100	100
$Feedback_{j \rightarrow i}$	[3 ... 5]	[3 ... 5]	[1 ... 2]	[1 ... 2]
$MaxAvgFeedback_i$	5	5	5	5
$MinAvgFeedback_i$	1	1	1	1
PA_i	1	0	1	0
QA_i	[0,1]	0	[0, 1]	0
CO_i	[0.5,1]	[0, 0.5)	[0.5, 1]	[0, 0.5)
$\alpha_1, \alpha_2, \alpha_3$	[0,1]	[0, 1]	[0, 1]	[0, 1]
$Trust_{threshold}$	0.5	0.5	0.5	0.5
$Profit_i$ (the initial value is considered an investment)	100	100	100	100

scenario can represent mistrusted CSPs (due to loss of customer data), but it is located in a country with high data protection quality. In both cases, this CSP could not gain a high level of CSP trust.

Scenario 4 - Low feedback with low institutional quality index: This scenario represents a CSP that has neither a high reputation level nor is located in a country with high institutional quality.

5   Result and Discussion

The analysis of the proposed trust model was performed utilizing the scenarios as shown in Table 1. The agent's settings are presented as shown in the above table. The scenarios are analyzed with respect to the profit of CSPs after CF has been established. The analysis was performed utilizing the global trust model (proposed trust model) and was compared with the CSP trust that does not consider an institutional trust. Global trust contains CSP Trust along with Institutional Trust. However, the CSP trust is the trust model that takes only feedback from the peer providers and does not consider an institutional trust. This comparison is utilized, in order to study the effect of trust with and without the presence of institutional trust on CF. It will help to give insight into how institutional trust affects CF formation for future studies.

Scenario one result shows that CSPs, who obtained high feedback with a high institutional quality index, can establish a cloud federation with every CSP that has an equivalent CSP feedback and institutional quality index. As a result, a CF is established by connecting with every agent, as these agents earn a high level of CSP trust from peer providers and are located in countries with uniform standards of data protection policy and with a strong cyber security strategy [39]. Once the participating CSPs have a uniform data protection strategy and strong cyber security strategy, the cloud federation can be established by evaluating only the CSP trust. Therefore, the CSPs located in a country with a high institutional quality index can be evaluated based on only their reputation level. As the simulation shows, the CF established utilizing global trust has an equivalent profit graph compared with the CF established utilizing only CSP trust.

Scenario two establishes a federation with CSPs, which have high feedback with a low institutional quality index. The proposed trust evaluation model excludes the CSPs with medium CSP trust (the value close to the threshold) and establishes a CF with a CSP with a very high level of feedback since the low institutional quality index decreases the level of Global trust. Therefore, in this scenario, the CSPs which have a very high level of feedback can establish a CF and produce an equivalent profit level as compared to the model that utilizes only CSP's feedback level. This implies that the CSP located in a low institutional quality country needs to earn a very high level of CSP trust so that they can establish cloud federations with other equivalent or more trustworthy CSPs (Table 2).

Table 2. Simulation result for profit for all 4 scenarios is compared with CSP Trust.

	High Institutional quality index	Low Institutional quality index
High Feedback		
Low Feedback		

As scenario three considers agents with a high institutional quality index but low CSP trust, this scenario represents new entrant CSPs to the market which does not accumulate enough trust from the society but are located in high institutional quality countries. In this case, the proposed model allows CSPs located in countries with a very high level of institutional quality to establish CF with the guarantee of their institutional quality. As the simulation result shows that CSPs, who join the CF can generate more profit. However, the model that utilizes only CSP trust will not allow the CSP to join a cloud federation and profit from it.

The last scenario considers low CSP trust with low institutional quality. This shows that risky CSPs in terms of data protection and trustable CSPs cannot establish CFs and profit from them. Given that, both models restrict the risky agents to establish CF.

6   Conclusion and Future Work

The aim of this study has been to propose a trust evaluation model, which considers CSP trust and institutional trust separately and utilizes them to compute global trust. In the international trade discipline, the concept of knowing a CSP's country data protection status is an early prediction mechanism of future trusted partner selections and cooperations. As CF is a cross-border international trade, this paper intended to show the impact of this concept, using a trust evaluation model. Moreover, the paper evaluates CSP trust with and without institutional trust.

The simulation result shows that during low institutional trust with high CSP trust, the proposed model establishes cloud federation with a low number of CSPs only, namely those who have the highest CSP trust level. This scenario shows that earning a very high level of trust from peer providers will guarantee CSPs with varying institutional trust to build CFs. In the case of low CSP trust with high institutional quality, the proposed model establishes a CF with CSPs with a high level of institutional quality. This scenario shows that new entrant CSP located in a country with high institutional quality can join a cloud federation with the guarantee of their institutional trust. There is no profit generated in the fourth scenario. Therefore, the effect of institutional quality is observed, if high institutional quality comes along with low CSP trust or if low institutional quality comes with high CSP trust.

For future work, the CSPs' opinions and confidence levels need to be included in the analysis. Using the confidence level and opinion of CSPs toward peer providers, a stability analysis can be performed.

Acknowledgment. This research was supported by the BK21 FOUR (Fostering Outstanding Universities for Research) funded by the Ministry of Education (MOE, Korea). This work was supported by the National Research Foundation of Korea (NRF) grant funded by the Korea government (MSIT) (No. NRF-2022R1A2C1092077).

References

1. Bañares, J.Á., Altmann, J.: Economics behind ICT infrastructure management. Electron. Mark. **28**(1), 7–9 (2018). https://doi.org/10.1007/s12525-018-0288-3

2. Haile, N., Altmann, J.: Evaluating investments in portability and interoperability between software service platforms. Futur. Gener. Comput. Syst. **78**, 224–241 (2018). https://doi.org/10.1016/j.future.2017.04.040

3. Haile, N., Altmann, J.: Structural analysis of value creation in software service platforms. Electron. Mark. **26**(2), 129–142 (2015). https://doi.org/10.1007/s12525-015-0208-8

4. Mahmood, Z.: Data location and security issues in cloud computing. In: 2011 International Conference on Emerging Intelligent Data and Web Technologies, Tirana, Albania, pp. 49–54 (2011). https://doi.org/10.1109/EIDWT.2011.16

5. Abu-Nusair, H.S.M.: Data location compliance in cloud computing (Jordan case study). M.C.S., Princess Sumaya University for Technology (Jordan), Jordan (2013). https://www.proquest.com/docview/2570578478/abstract/28572B03CACB40E0PQ/1. Accessed 15 Aug 2022

6. Noltes, J.: Data location compliance in cloud computing (2011). https://essay.utwente.nl/61042/. Accessed 15 Aug 2022

7. Gebrealif, Y., Mubarkoot, M., Altmann, J., Egger, B.: AI-based container orchestration for federated cloud environments. In: Proceedings of the 1st Workshop on Flexible Resource and Application Management on the Edge, Virtual Event Sweden, pp. 15–16 (2020). https://doi.org/10.1145/3452369.3463818

8. Haile, N., Altmann, J.: Risk-Benefit-Mediated Impact of Determinants on the Adoption of Cloud Federation. Seoul National University; Technology Management, Economics, and Policy … (2015)

9. Jeferry, K., et al.: Challenges emerging from future cloud application scenarios. Procedia Comput. Sci. **68**, 227–237 (2015). https://doi.org/10.1016/j.procs.2015.09.238

10. Altmann, J., et al.: BASMATI - A Brokerage Architecture on Federated Clouds for Mobile Applications. Seoul National University; Technology Management, Economics, and Policy Program (TEMEP), 2016132 (2016). https://ideas.repec.org/p/snv/dp2009/2016132.html. Accessed 21 Sept 2022

11. Aryal, R.G., Marshall, J., Altmann, J.: Architecture and business logic specification for dynamic cloud federations. In: Djemame, K., Altmann, J., Bañares, J.Á., Agmon Ben-Yehuda, O., Naldi, M. (eds.) GECON 2019. LNCS, vol. 11819, pp. 83–96. Springer, Cham (2019). https://doi.org/10.1007/978-3-030-36027-6_8

12. Aryal, R.G., Altmann, J.: Fairness in revenue sharing for stable cloud federations. In: Pham, C., Altmann, J., Bañares, J.Á. (eds.) GECON 2017. LNCS, vol. 10537, pp. 219–232. Springer, Cham (2017). https://doi.org/10.1007/978-3-319-68066-8_17

13. Kanwal, A., Masood, R., Shibli, M.A.: Evaluation and establishment of trust in cloud federation (2014). https://www.scopus.com/inward/record.uri?eid=2-s2.0-84899760598&doi=10.1145%2f2557977.2558023&partnerID=40&md5=37391e418deea959a3235e24dcd1ad10

14. Gebrealif, Y., Mubarkoot, M., Altmann, J., Egger, B.: Architecture for orchestrating containers in cloud federations. In: Tserpes, K., et al. (eds.) GECON 2021. LNCS, vol. 13072, pp. 66–75. Springer, Cham (2021). https://doi.org/10.1007/978-3-030-92916-9_6

15. Mellaoui, W., Posso, R., Gebrealif, Y., Bock, E., Altmann, J., Yoon, H.: Knowledge management framework for cloud federation. In: Tserpes, K., et al. (eds.) GECON 2021. LNCS, vol. 13072, pp. 123–132. Springer, Cham (2021). https://doi.org/10.1007/978-3-030-92916-9_10

16. Yu, S., Beugelsdijk, S., de Haan, J.: Trade, trust and the rule of law. Eur. J. Polit. Econ. **37**, 102–115 (2015). https://doi.org/10.1016/j.ejpoleco.2014.11.003

17. Kim, D.J., Song, Y.I., Braynov, S.B., Rao, H.R.: A multidimensional trust formation model in B-to-C e-commerce: a conceptual framework and content analyses of academia/practitioner perspectives. Decis. Support Syst. **40**(2), 143–165 (2005). https://doi.org/10.1016/j.dss.2004.01.006

18. Naseer, M.K., Jabbar, S., Zafar, I.: A novel trust model for selection of cloud service provider. In: 2014 World Symposium on Computer Applications & Research (WSCAR), Sousse, Tunisia, pp. 1–6 (2014). https://doi.org/10.1109/WSCAR.2014.6916772

19. Derahman, M.N., Abdullah, A., Azmi, M.F.: Robust reputation based trust management framework for federated-cloud environments. Int. J. Appl. Eng. Res. (2016). https://www.scopus.com/inward/record.uri?eid=2-s2.0-85026679266&partnerID=40&md5=cd0a8910e1b1bc4e81a6e4f3a89677c8

20. Mashayekhy, L., Nejad, M.M., Grosu, D.: A trust-aware mechanism for cloud federation formation. IEEE Trans. Cloud Comput. 9(4), 1278–1292 (2021). https://doi.org/10.1109/TCC.2019.2911831

21. Papadakis-Vlachopapadopoulos, K., González, R.S., Dimolitsas, I., Dechouniotis, D., Ferrer, A.J., Papavassiliou, S.: Collaborative SLA and reputation-based trust management in cloud federations. Future Gener. Comput. Syst. 100, 498–512 (2019). https://doi.org/10.1016/j.future.2019.05.030

22. Gupta, M.K., Annappa, B.: Trusted partner selection in broker based cloud federation. In: 2016 International Conference on Next Generation Intelligent Systems (ICNGIS), pp. 1–6 (2016)

23. Hadjres, S., Belqasmi, F., El Barachi, M., Kara, N.: A green, energy, and trust-aware multi-objective cloud coalition formation approach. Futur. Gener. Comput. Syst. 111, 52–67 (2020)

24. Abawajy, J.: Establishing trust in hybrid cloud computing environments (2011). https://www.scopus.com/inward/record.uri?eid=2-s2.0-84856193158&doi=10.1109%2fTrustCom.2011.18&partnerID=40&md5=1a68b3a35d726252e03d2f5597fccfb3

25. Ray, B., Saha, A., Khatua, S., Roy, S.: Quality and profit assured trusted cloud federation formation: Game theory based approach. IEEE Trans. Serv. Comput. 14, 805–819 (2018)

26. Dhole, A., Thomas, M.V., Chandrasekaran, K.: An efficient trust-based game-theoretic approach for cloud federation formation. In: 2016 3rd International Conference on Advanced Computing and Communication Systems (ICACCS), vol. 1, pp. 1–6 (2016)

27. Kurdi, H., Alshayban, B., Altoaimy, L., Alsalamah, S.: TrustyFeer: a subjective logic trust model for smart city peer-to-peer federated clouds. Wirel. Commun. Mob. Comput. (2018). https://www.scopus.com/inward/record.uri?eid=2-s2.0-85044051077&doi=10.1155%2f2018%2f1073216&partnerID=40&md5=6b03461200de220697a740f9a23b12e0

28. Latif, R., Afzaal, S.H., Latif, S.: A novel cloud management framework for trust establishment and evaluation in a federated cloud environment. J. Supercomput. (2021). https://www.scopus.com/inward/record.uri?eid=2-s2.0-85104130905&doi=10.1007%2fs11227-021-03775-8&partnerID=40&md5=9352984d5a89e149390a2df92c88a34b

29. Ahmed, U., Raza, I., Hussain, S.A.: Trust evaluation in cross-cloud federation: survey and requirement analysis. ACM Comput. Surv. 52(1) (2019). https://doi.org/10.1145/3292499

30. Ghafoorian, M., Abbasinezhad-Mood, D., Shakeri, H.: A thorough trust and reputation based RBAC model for secure data storage in the cloud. IEEE Trans. Parallel Distrib. Syst. 30(4), 778–788 (2019). https://doi.org/10.1109/TPDS.2018.2870652

31. Hassan, M.M., et al.: QoS and trust-aware coalition formation game in data-intensive cloud federations. Concurr. Comput. Pract. Experience 28(10), 2889–2905 (2016)

32. Breskovic, I., Altmann, J., Brandic, I.: Creating standardized products for electronic markets. Futur. Gener. Comput. Syst. 29(4), 1000–1011 (2013). https://doi.org/10.1016/j.future.2012.06.007

33. Ahmed, U., Raza, I., Rana, O.F., Hussain, S.A.: Aggregated capability assessment (AgCA) for CAIQ enabled cross-cloud Federation. IEEE Trans. Serv. Comput. 15(5), 2619–2632 (2022). https://doi.org/10.1109/TSC.2021.3073783

34. Aryal, R.G., Altmann, J.: Dynamic application deployment in federations of clouds and edge resources using a multiobjective optimization AI algorithm. In: 2018 Third International

Conference on Fog and Mobile Edge Computing (FMEC), Barcelona, pp. 147–154 (2018). https://doi.org/10.1109/FMEC.2018.8364057

35. Romero Coronado, J.P., Altmann, J.: Model for incentivizing cloud service federation (2017). https://www.scopus.com/inward/record.uri?eid=2-s2.0-85032482917&doi=10.1007%2f978-3-319-68066-8_18&partnerID=40&md5=615fdbddf64814dfbe3445960676535b
36. Hofman, D., Duranti, L., How, E.: Trust in the balance: data protection laws as tools for privacy and security in the cloud. Algorithms **10**(2), 47 (2017). https://doi.org/10.3390/a10020047
37. von Grafenstein, M.: Co-regulation and competitive advantage in the GDPR: data protection certification mechanisms, codes of conduct and data protection-by-design. In: Research Handbook on Privacy and Data Protection Law, pp. 402–432 (2022)
38. Krishna, B., Krishnan, S., Sebastian, M.P.: Examining the relationship between national cybersecurity commitment, culture, and digital payment usage: an institutional trust theory perspective. Inf. Syst. Front. (2022). https://doi.org/10.1007/s10796-022-10280-7
39. Kim, K., Altmann, J.: Effect of homophily on network formation. Commun. Nonlinear Sci. Numer. Simul. **44**, 482–494 (2017). https://doi.org/10.1016/j.cnsns.2016.08.011

A Game-Theoretic Approach for Pricing and Determining Virtual Reality Investment and Cybersecurity Level in a Dual-Channel Supply Chain

Amir Mohammad Alaei[1], Morteza Rasti-Barzoki[1,2,3]([⊠]), Jörn Altmann[2,3], and Bernhard Egger[4]

[1] Department of Industrial and Systems Engineering, Isfahan University of Technology, 84156-83111 Isfahan, Iran
a.m.alaei1373@ut.ac.ir, rasti@cc.iut.ac.ir
[2] Institute of Engineering Research, College of Engineering, Seoul National University, Seoul 08826, South Korea
jorn.altmann@acm.org
[3] Technology Management Economics and Policy Program, College of Engineering, Seoul National University, Seoul 08826, South Korea
[4] Department of Computer Science and Engineering, College of Engineering, Seoul National University, Seoul 08826, South Korea
bernhard@csap.snu.ac.kr

Abstract. Virtual reality has become a new option to inform the customers about product before purchasing. However, providing virtual reality may create new challenges. For instance, consumers may obtain essential information about products by using virtual reality option, but eventually they buy their products from the offline channel. This phenomenon is called webrooming. Another challenge is cyber-attacks. E-tailers and their consumers face risks from cyber-attacks. Thus, e-tailers are investing to improve cybersecurity. We consider a dual-channel supply chain consisting of an offline retailer and an e-tailer who purchase the same product from a manufacturer at the same wholesale price. The e-tailer offers a partial refund policy in order to attract the customers. Also, to reduce consumer valuation uncertainty, the e-tailer faces the decision on whether to introduce virtual reality. We analyze three scenarios. Firstly, the e-tailer does not offer virtual reality. Secondly, the e-tailer offers virtual reality, but he does not invest on cybersecurity. Thirdly, the e-tailer offers virtual reality and invests on cybersecurity.

Keywords: Game theory · Pricing · Virtual reality · Cybersecurity · Webrooming · Return policy

1 Introduction

Nowadays, online selling is more popular than ever. E-commerce has made it easy to buy everything and consumers can easily order the required product with a click. According

J. Á. Bañares et al. (Eds.): GECON 2022, LNCS 13430, pp. 62–71, 2023.
https://doi.org/10.1007/978-3-031-29315-3_6

to Statista website, online selling was almost 4938 billion U.S. dollars worldwide in 2021 and it will grow 15.9% in the United States in 2022. However, obtaining enough information about the products in online shopping is more complex than in offline shopping. Virtual reality (VR) has become interesting tool for e-tailers to inform customers about the product in online channels. By using VR, customers can imagine themselves in the store environment and get enough information about the product. eBay is one of the e-tailers that provides VR on its website and customers can experience the store atmosphere virtually [1].

However, VR can create challenges and concerns for e-tailers. Webrooming behavior is one of the new challenges of VR; means consumers use VR in online channel to obtain required information, but switch to offline channel and buy through offline retailers [2]. Google has done a survey that shows 87% of people begin product search online, but 79% purchase their product in physical stores [3]. Evidently, consumer webrooming behavior causes consumers to switch from online to offline, which may decrease the online demand and increase price competition. Thus, e-tailers should carefully decide on whether to provide VR.

Another challenge of online sales channels and using new technologies in online channels is cyber-attacks. Although online shopping is easier for people, many consumers are afraid of stealing their information when shopping online. Thus, cybersecurity has come to the attention of e-tailers and is now a global priority.

Many researchers study the influence of showrooming in supply chain [4–8]. Their findings show that the showrooming hurt the physical retailer and reduces the retailer's profit. On contrary, the effect of webrooming has been studied less in literature. Jing [2] examined the interaction between webrooming and showrooming. He shows that when webrooming reduces online purchasing uncertainty, it benefits both offline retailer and e-tailer by persuading more consumers to participate. Sun, Wang [9] analyzed the cost of searching online and demonstrated that consumer webrooming behavior depends on the cost of searching online and the travel cost of visiting physical stores. Sun, Wang [3] proposed a model consisting of a manufacturer and a retailer to examine the optimal webrooming strategy. Their results show that the optimal webrooming strategy depended on the online shopping cost. Jiao and Hu [10] proposed a model with different information of product value that consumers can obtain by referring to a traditional retailer and researching from an e-tailer, and studied consumer showrooming/webrooming behavior in a single model. Their results show that showrooming/webrooming may benefit traditional retailers and e-tailers, respectively. Domina, Lee [11] concluded that the enjoyment of using VR for customers increases demand and purchases. Gabisch [12] found that the experience of the virtual store leads to the intention of visiting the physical stores and shopping behavior. In food industry, Pizzi, Scarpi [13] and van Herpen, van den Broek [14] examined and compared shopping through a store with the possibility of VR and physical store and stated that the experience of buying from a store with VR can lead to customer satisfaction.

As far as we know, there are no studies that consider virtual reality investment in a dual-channel supply chain in the presence of webrooming behavior. Also, addressing the issue of cybersecurity and the investment of e-tailer on cybersecurity is of particular importance. In this paper, we consider a dual-channel supply chain consisting of one e-tailer and one offline retailer wherein the e-tailer decides whether to provide virtual reality. We examine the optimal virtual reality investment by considering the webrooming effect and the effect of virtual reality on return function. Also, we investigate the cybersecurity level when the e-tailer decides to provide virtual reality. We analyze three scenarios. Firstly, the e-tailer does not offer virtual reality. Secondly, the e-tailer offers virtual reality, but he does not invest on cybersecurity. Thirdly, the e-tailer offers virtual reality and invests on cybersecurity. The important questions are as follows:

(1) what are the equilibrium prices under each scenario?
(2) what is the equilibrium virtual reality investment?
(3) what is the optimal cybersecurity level when the e-tailer provides virtual reality?
(4) what is the effect of virtual reality on product return function?

The remain of this research is organized as follows. Section 2 present problem definition. Section 3 provides the equilibrium results for each scenario. Section 4 discuss a numerical example with important results. Finally, Sect. 5 provides the conclusion.

2 Problem Description

We consider a dual-channel supply chain consisting of an online and an offline retailer who purchase the same product at the same wholesale price, and sell the product through online and offline channels, respectively. Because the consumers who buy through online channel are not able to test the product before buying, the e-tailer utilizes two strategies to compete with the offline retailer and attract customers. First, the e-tailer offers partial refund policy to create confidence for online consumers. Second, since the online consumers are not able to test the product before purchasing, the e-tailer decides whether to provide virtual reality. Providing virtual reality allows consumers to be fully aware of the product before purchasing and may reduce the return rate. But on the other hand, it may lead to webrooming behavior and reduces the demand of online channel. Another issue that may threaten e-tailer is cybersecurity. By offering virtual reality, the e-tailer should also pay special attention to cybersecurity. Therefore, by providing virtual reality, the e-tailer also decides on the level of cybersecurity. In this paper, we use Stackelberg game model to formulate the relationship between the retailers. The offline retailer is leader and the e-tailer acts as follower. At first, the offline retailer decides his retail price. Then, the e-tailer determines the online retail price, virtual reality investment and cybersecurity level.

2.1 Scenario 1

In this scenario, the e-tailer offers partial refund policy and does not provide virtual reality; that is $v = 0$. The offline retailer firstly determines his retail price and then the e-tailer decides online retail price. The optimal model is as follows:

$$\max_{p_d^1} \pi_d^1 = \left(p_d^1 - w\right) \underbrace{\left(1 - \alpha_r - \beta p_d + \gamma p_r\right)}_{D_d^1}$$

$$\text{s.t. } \max_{p_r^1} \pi_r^1 = \left(p_r^1 - w\right) \underbrace{\left(\alpha_r - \beta p_r + \gamma p_d\right)}_{D_r^1} - r \underbrace{\left(\theta + \omega r\right)}_{R^1} \tag{1}$$

where α_r is market potential in online channel, β and γ represent sensitivity of product demand to the price of own and another channel, respectively. $\theta + \omega r$ indicates the return function of the product, wherein θ is basic return of product that does not depends on its refund amount, ω is sensitivity of returns quantity with respect to refund amount, and r is refund amount of a unit product.

2.2 Scenario 2

Under scenario 2, in addition to offering partial refund policy, the e-tailer provides virtual reality in online channel; that is $v > 0$. First, the offline retailer decides retail price in offline channel. Next, the e-tailer determine the online retail price and virtual reality investment. The formulation of optimal model is:

$$\max_{p_d^2} \pi_d^2 = \left(p_d^2 - w\right) \underbrace{\left(1 - \alpha_r - \beta p_d^2 + \gamma p_r^2 + (1 - \varepsilon_r)v^2\right)}_{D_d^2}$$

$$\text{s.t. } \max_{p_r^2, v^2} \pi_r^2 = \left(p_r^2 - w\right) \underbrace{\left(\alpha_r - \beta p_r^2 + \gamma p_d^2 + \varepsilon_r v^2\right)}_{D_r^2} - r \underbrace{\left(\theta + \omega r - \lambda v^2\right)}_{R^2} - \frac{1}{2}v^2 \tag{2}$$

where ε_r refers to virtual reality effect coefficient in online channel, v is virtual reality investment that is a decision variable, and λ is sensitivity of returns quantity with respect to virtual reality investment.

2.3 Scenario 3

In scenario 3, the possibility of a cyber-attack has been seen in the online channel. The e-tailer decides the cybersecurity level in this scenario. The probability of a successful cyber-attack is $n = 1 - z$, that z is cybersecurity level. The total number of website shutdown is $Q = n \times f$, that f refers to total number of cyber-attacks. The model of third scenario is as follows:

$$\max_{p_d^3} \pi_d^3 = \left(p_d^3 - w\right) \underbrace{\left(1 - \alpha_r - \beta p_d^3 + \gamma p_r^3 + (1 - \varepsilon_r)v^3\right)}_{D_d^3}$$

$$s.t. \max_{p_r^3, v^3, z^3} \pi_r^3 = \left(p_r^3 - w\right) \underbrace{\left(\alpha_r - \beta p_r^3 + \gamma p_d^3 + \varepsilon_r v^3 - \mu Q\right)}_{D_r^3} - r \underbrace{\left(\theta + \omega r - \lambda v^3\right)}_{R^3}$$

$$- (Q \times k) - \frac{1}{2}v^3 - \frac{1}{2}z^3$$

$$(3)$$

where parameter μ indicates sensitivity of product demand to cybersecurity level and k represents cost of website shutdown.

3 Equilibrium Solutions

3.1 Scenario 1

Lemma 1. π_r^1 on p_r^1 and π_d^1 on p_d^1 are concave functions.

Proof. Taking the second derivative of Eq. (1) with respect to p_r^1 and p_d^1, we have $-2\beta < 0$ and $-2\beta + \frac{\gamma^2}{\beta} < 0$. Therefore, the profit functions under scenario 1 are concave.

Theorem 1. *Under scenario 1, the equilibrium prices of the two retailers are:*

$$p_r^1 = \beta w + 2\beta\left(\alpha_r + \gamma\left((\gamma - 2\beta)\alpha_r + \beta(2 + \gamma w)/2\left(2\beta^2 - \gamma^2\right) + 0.5w\right)\right) \quad (4)$$

$$p_d^1 = \frac{(\gamma - 2\beta)\alpha_r + \beta(2 + \gamma w)}{2(2\beta^2 - \gamma^2)} + \frac{w}{2} \quad (5)$$

3.2 Scenario 2

Lemma 2. π_r^2 on p_r^2 and v and π_d^2 on p_d^2 are jointly concave functions.

Proof. The Hessian matrix for π_r^2 is calculated as $H = \begin{pmatrix} -2\beta & \varepsilon_r \\ \varepsilon_r & -1 \end{pmatrix}$ that is negative definite. Thus, π_r^2 in Eq. (2) is jointly concave in p_r^2 and v^2. Hence, by setting $\partial \pi_r^2/\partial p_r = 0$ and $\partial \pi_r^2/\partial v = 0$, the unique optimal set (p_r^2, v^2) is obtained. Now, after substituting Eqs. (6) and (7) in Eq. (2), the second derivative of π_d^2 in Eq. (2) with respect to p_d^2 is $-2\beta + \left(2\varepsilon_r\gamma - 2\varepsilon_r^2\gamma + 2\gamma^2/2\beta - \varepsilon_r^2\right) < 0$.

Theorem 2. *Under scenario 2, the equilibrium solutions of the two retailers are:*

$$p_r^2 = \frac{\alpha_r - w\beta + \varepsilon_r \lambda r + \gamma p_d^2}{2\beta - \varepsilon_r^2} + w \tag{6}$$

$$v^2 = \frac{2\beta\lambda r + \varepsilon_r(\alpha_r - \beta w + \gamma p_d^2)}{2\beta - \varepsilon_r^2} \tag{7}$$

$$p_d^2 = 2\beta(1 - \alpha_r) + \varepsilon_r(\alpha_r - (\beta + \gamma)w - \varepsilon_r) \\ - w\frac{(\gamma^2 + \beta(\gamma + 2\beta)) + \lambda r(2\beta(1 - \varepsilon_r) + \gamma\varepsilon_r)}{2\beta(2\beta - \varepsilon_r^2) + 2\gamma\varepsilon_r^2 - 2\varepsilon_r\gamma - 2\gamma^2} \tag{8}$$

3.3 Scenario 3

Lemma 3. π_r^3 *on* p_r^3, v, *and* z *and* π_d^3 *on* p_d^3 *are jointly concave functions.*

Proof. The Hessian matrix for π_r^3 is calculated as $H = \begin{pmatrix} -2\beta & \varepsilon_r & \mu f \\ \varepsilon_r & -1 & 0 \\ \mu f & 0 & -1 \end{pmatrix}$ that is
negative definite. Thus, π_r^3 in Eq. (3) is jointly concave in p_r^3, v^3, and z^3. Hence, by setting
$\partial\pi_r^3/\partial p_r = 0$, $\partial\pi_r^3/\partial v = 0$, and $\partial\pi_r^3/\partial z = 0$, the unique optimal set (p_r^3, v^3, z^3) is
obtained. Now, after substituting Eqs. (9), (10), and (11) in Eq. (3), the second derivative
of π_d^3 in Eq. (3) with respect to p_d^3 is $-2\beta - \frac{-2\varepsilon_r^2\gamma + 2\varepsilon_r\gamma + 2\gamma^2}{\varepsilon_r^2 + f^2\mu^2 - 2\beta} < 0$.

Theorem 3. *Under scenario 3, the equilibrium solutions of the two retailers are:*

$$p_r^3 = \alpha_r - \mu f + k\mu f^2 - \varepsilon_r \lambda r + \beta w + \gamma p_d^3 - w\left(\varepsilon_r^2 + \mu^2 f^2\right)/\varepsilon_r^2 - 2\beta + (\mu f)^2 \tag{9}$$

$$v^3 = \lambda r(\mu f)^2 + \varepsilon_r\left(\alpha\|r + \beta w + \gamma p_d^3 + \mu f - k\mu f^2\right) + 2\beta\lambda r/\varepsilon_r^2 - 2\beta + (\mu f)^2 \tag{10}$$

$$z^3 = -f\left(2\beta k + \alpha_r\mu - k\varepsilon_r^2 - f\mu^2 + \gamma\mu p_d^3 - \beta\mu w + \varepsilon_r\mu\lambda r\right)/\varepsilon_r^2 - 2\beta + (\mu f)^2 \tag{11}$$

$$p_d^3 = \frac{\begin{array}{c}(\mu f)^2(1 - \alpha_r + \lambda r(1 - \varepsilon_r) + w(\beta + \gamma)) + (\alpha_r + \beta w - \gamma w - \mu f)(\varepsilon_r) \\ + 2\beta(1 - \alpha_r + \beta w) + \varepsilon_r^2(\mu f - 1) \\ + \mu f^2(k\varepsilon_r(1 - \varepsilon_r) + \gamma) + \lambda r(\varepsilon_r\gamma - 2\beta\varepsilon_r + 2\beta)\end{array}}{2(\beta\varepsilon_r^2 - \varepsilon_r^2\gamma + \varepsilon_r\gamma + \beta(\mu f)^2 - 2\beta^2 + \gamma^2)} \tag{12}$$

4 Numerical Example

In this section, due to the complexity of equations and optimal solutions, we use a numerical example to compare the optimal solutions in three scenarios. Following Zhang, Chen [15] and Li, Li [4], the parameters are setting as $\alpha_r = 0.6$, $\beta = 0.5$, $\gamma = 0.1$, $\mu = 0.2$, $w = 0.6$, $\varepsilon_r = 0.5$, $\theta = 0.02$, $\omega = 0.005$, $\lambda = 0.008$, $r = 0.5$ and $k = 2$.

Figure 1 shows that a higher webrooming effect coefficient will increase the equilibrium retail prices in both online and offline channels. The reason behind this is that the impact of webrooming increases the number of potential customers and thus increases market demand. Therefore, both retailers increase retail prices to obtain more profit. With the increase of webrooming effect, the slope of offline retailer price increase is higher than the slope of e-tailer price increase, which shows that offline retailer benefits more from virtual reality without any payment for virtual reality with increased demand and consequently rising prices.

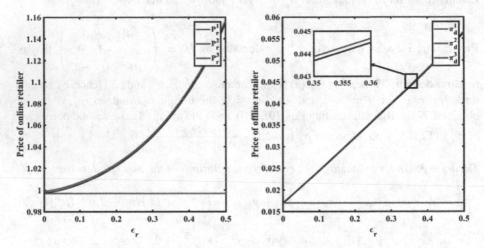

Fig. 1. Optimal prices comparison.

Figure 2 indicates that a higher webrooming effect coefficient increases the profits of both retailers. This suggests that although providing virtual reality may lead to webrooming behavior and reduces e-tailer's demand, it is not always harmful to the e-tailer and, as we can see in the Fig. 2, always increases the profitability of both retailers.

Figure 3 illustrates the changes of virtual reality investment and return function with respect to virtual reality effect coefficient and sensitivity of returns quantity with respect to virtual reality investment. The higher the sensitivity of the return function on the virtual reality investment and the higher the webrooming effect coefficient, the greater the e-tailer investing on virtual reality, and the return function decreases. Therefore, in answer to question 4, we can say that with the increase of e-tailer's investment on virtual reality, customers become fully aware of the product, and the number of returned products decreases.

Figure 4 shows that increasing the sensitivity of product demand to the cybersecurity level leads to increasing the cybersecurity level and decreasing the virtual reality investment. The reason for this is that as demand sensitivity to cybersecurity level increases, the e-tailer decides to focus more on cybersecurity instead of increasing their investment on virtual reality. That is, increase investment on cybersecurity by reducing investment on virtual reality.

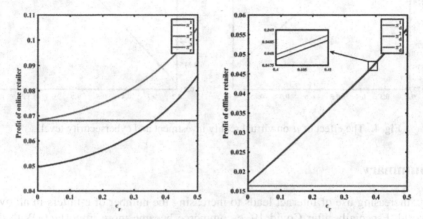

Fig. 2. Equilibrium profits comparison.

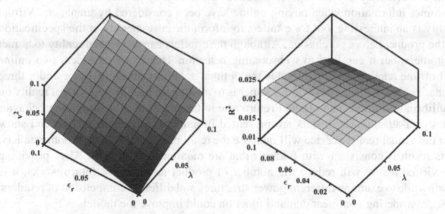

Fig. 3. The effect of ε_r and λ on virtual reality investment and return function.

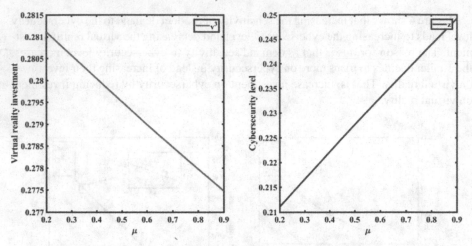

Fig. 4. The effect of μ on virtual reality investment and cybersecurity level.

5 Summary

Today, increasing use of Internet leads to increasing the number of e-tailers in all over the world. Especially after Covid 19, e-commerce became more important. With the increasing importance of e-commerce and the increase in the number of e-tailers, issues such as reviewing and testing the product before buying online, and the security of customer information when buying online have been considered by managers. Virtual reality is an interesting tool for e-tailers to inform the customer about the specification of the product before purchasing. Although the e-tailers can use virtual reality to attract customers, but it can lead to webrooming behavior. This paper considers two online and offline retailers and investigates the optimal solutions of each retailer under three scenarios. The main purpose of this paper is to investigate the effect of virtual reality on equilibrium solutions and product return rate in the presence of webrooming behavior and cyber-attacks. The results are presented in numerical example section and show that the virtual reality service will increase the retail prices and profits of both retailers. This result is consistent with findings that are mentioned in [4, 15]. Also, providing the virtual reality will reduce the number of product retuned. For future works, it is worthwhile to examine different power structures and different competition of retailers. Also, considering nonlinear demand function could improve the model.

Acknowledgements. This work was supported by the Korean Ministry of Science and ICT through the National Research Foundation (NRF) of Korea grant No. NRF-2022R1A2C1092077, and, also, by NRF grants 0536-20210093 and 21A20151113068 (BK21 Plus for Pioneers in Innovative Computing - Dept. of Computer Science and Engineering, SNU). The Institute of Engineering Research (IOER) and the Institute of Computer Technology (ICT) at Seoul National University provided research facilities for this study.

References

1. Jin, B., Kim, G., Moore, M., Rothenberg, L.: Consumer store experience through virtual reality: its effect on emotional states and perceived store attractiveness. Fashion Text. **8**(1), 1–21 (2021). https://doi.org/10.1186/s40691-021-00256-7
2. Jing, B.: Showrooming and webrooming: information externalities between online and offline sellers. Mark. Sci. **37**(3), 469–483 (2018)
3. Sun, Y., et al.: Digital showroom strategies for dual-channel supply chains in the presence of consumer webrooming behavior.Ann. Oper. Res. 1–40 (2022)
4. Li, G., Li, L., Sun, J.: Pricing and service effort strategy in a dual-channel supply chain with showrooming effect. Transp. Res. Part E: Logistics Transp. Rev. **126**, 32–48 (2019)
5. Li, M., Zhang, X., Dan, B.: Competition and cooperation in a supply chain with an offline showroom under asymmetric information. Int. J. Prod. Res. **58**(19), 5964–5979 (2020)
6. Mehra, A., Kumar, S., Raju, J.S.: Competitive strategies for brick-and-mortar stores to counter "showrooming." Manage. Sci. **64**(7), 3076–3090 (2018)
7. Mitra, S.: Economic models of price competition between traditional and online retailing under showrooming. Decision **49**(1), 29–63 (2022)
8. Wang, S., Luo, T., Chang, D.: Pricing strategies of multichannel apparel supply chain based on showrooming and information sharing. Math. Probl. Eng., 1–23 (2021)
9. Sun, Y., Wang, Z., Han, X.: Supply chain channel strategies for online retailers: whether to introduce web showrooms? Transp. Res. Part E: Logistics Transp. Rev. **144**, 102122 (2020)
10. Jiao, C., Hu, B.: Showrooming, webrooming, and operational strategies for competitiveness. Prod. Oper. Manage. **31**(8), 3217–3232 (2021)
11. Domina, T., Lee, S.-E., MacGillivray, M.: Understanding factors affecting consumer intention to shop in a virtual world. J. Retail. Consum. Serv. **19**(6), 613–620 (2012)
12. Gabisch, J.A.: Virtual world brand experience and its impact on real world purchasing behavior. J. Brand Manage. **19**(1), 18–32 (2011)
13. Pizzi, G., et al.: Virtual reality, real reactions?: Comparing consumers' perceptions and shopping orientation across physical and virtual-reality retail stores. Comput. Hum. Behav. **96**, 1–12 (2019)
14. van Herpen, E., et al.: Can a virtual supermarket bring realism into the lab? Comparing shopping behavior using virtual and pictorial store representations to behavior in a physical store. Appetite **107**, 196–207 (2016)
15. Zhang, X., et al.: Optimal showroom service strategy and power structure for retailers considering consumer return. Discrete Dyn. Nat. Soc. 1–22 (2021)

Serveless Computing, IoT, Edge, Resource Management

Semi-automated Capacity Analysis of Limitation-Aware Microservices Architectures

Rafael Fresno–Aranda(✉) [ID], Pablo Fernández [ID], Amador Durán [ID], and Antonio Ruiz–Cortés [ID]

SCORE Lab, I3US Institute, Universidad de Sevilla, Seville, Spain
{rfresno,pablofm,amador,aruiz}@us.es

Abstract. The so-called API economy has popularised the consumption of APIs and their payment through pricing plans. This trend is very much in line with and particularly beneficial for systems with a microservices architecture that makes use of external APIs. In these cases, more and more often, the design of the system is based on the premise that its functionality is offered to its users within certain operating conditions, which implies that its architecture is aware of both the plans of external APIs and its capacity limits. We have coined these architectures as limitation-aware microservices architectures (LAMA). Furthermore, in case of a Software as a Service (SaaS) model implemented with a LAMA, the operating conditions would be explicitly grounded in the specific plans agreed with the SaaS customers. In such a context, to design a set of potential pricing plans for the LAMA and predict the expected operating conditions, it is necessary to determine the capacity limits that the architecture will offer and the cost of using external API. This is a tedious, time-consuming, and error-prone activity, so its automation would be of great value to software architects.

In this paper, we coin the term LAMA, describe the problem of automated capacity analysis of LAMAs, present a first approach to solving it by interpreting it as an optimisation problem implementable as a constraint satisfaction and optimisation problem and introduce three basic analysis operations from which any number of other operations can be modelled. Finally, a tooling support is also introduced.

Keywords: Capacity Analysis · Microservices Architectures · API · Services · QoS

1 Introduction

The so-called *API economy* refers to an ecosystem of APIs used as business elements, where software system developers subscribe to and consume external APIs, while also providing their own APIs with their own pricing plans. WSO2 defines the API economy as *the ability for APIs to create new value and revenue streams for organisations through the use of APIs* [22]. Similarly, Capgemini defines it as *the ecosystem of business opportunities enabled by the delivery of functionality, data, and algorithms over APIs* [4]. Thus, the API economy has popularised the consumption of APIs and their payment through what are known as *pricing plans*, which describe their functionality, their capacity limits (aka limitations) and the price for using them.

The API economy is very much in line with and particularly beneficial for systems with a microservices architecture (MSA) [6] that uses external APIs. In an MSA, each microservice should have a well-defined API and make use of a standardized paradigm to integrate with the rest of microservices in the architecture and the external supporting services; usually, the most used paradigm used to define the interface and inter-operate is the RESTful paradigm.

More and more often, the design of the system is based on the premise that its functionality is offered to its users within certain operating conditions, which implies that its architecture is built and operated taking into consideration the limitations derived from its capacity and usage of external APIs. Note that for the remainder of this paper we will refer to the microservices of an architecture as **internal services**, even though they usually offer an API themselves; the term API will be reserved for **external APIs**.

Taking into consideration this common scenario in the industry, we aim to coin those architectures as *limitation-aware microservices architectures* (LAMA). In such a context, it is important to note that in the case of Software as a Service (SaaS) implemented with a LAMA, limitations play an even bigger role as the operating conditions would be explicitly grounded in the specific plans agreed with the SaaS customers. As an example, Fig. 1 shows a LAMA composed by three different services (S1, S2, S3) that make use of two external APIs (E1, E2) with different pricing plans. The LAMA customers have a pricing plan where they have to choose between the *Starter* plan and *Advanced* plan with different guaranteed operating conditions on the Requests Per Second (RPS) and a corresponding monthly price.

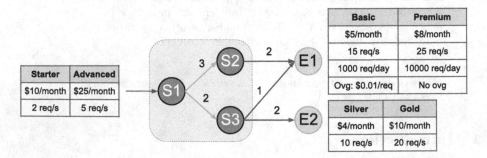

Starter	Advanced
$10/month	$25/month
2 req/s	5 req/s

Basic	Premium
$5/month	$8/month
15 req/s	25 req/s
1000 req/day	10000 req/day
Ovg: $0.01/req	No ovg

Silver	Gold
$4/month	$10/month
10 req/s	20 req/s

Fig. 1. A sample LAMA with 3 internal services and 2 external APIs, each of them with 2 pricing plans. Plan *Basic* has an overage cost. The LAMA offers its functionality through two pricing plans.

In order to design the LAMA pricing plans and predict the operating conditions, it is necessary to determine the capacity limits that the architecture will offer and the cost of using external APIs, analysing different scenarios; specifically, as motivating examples, we can identify three common situations: i) in order to articulate a strategic decision to define the LAMA pricing plan for a estimated scenario, we can ask about the baseline operational cost for such scenario (e.g. *Q1 - What is the cheapest operational cost for my LAMA in order to offer 2 RPS to 20 customers?*); ii) given a fixed relationship or a pre-existing ongoing contract with an external API, we could ask about the expected maximal operating conditions (e.g. *Q2 - Assuming we have a Basic plan and a Gold plan already contracted what is the maximal requests per minute (RPM) I can guarantee to all my 20 customers?*); iii) in case we have a pre-existing budget limit for a given scenario, we could ask about the optimal combination of plans to be subscribed and the potential limitations I could guarantee to my customers with this combination (e.g. *Q3 - Assuming we have a monthly budget limit of $120 in my LAMA, which is the maximum RPS to each of 20 customers?*).

Beyond SaaS, it is important to note that those motivating examples can also be adapted for any LAMA, even if they represent ad-hoc systems inside a single organization and the number of customers is not relevant for the calculations, for example: *Q4 - What is the cheapest operational cost to guarantee a global operating condition of 50 RPS?*, *Q5 - Assuming we have a Basic plan and a Gold plan already contracted what is the maximal RPS I can guarantee as operating condition?* or, *Q6 - Assuming we have a monthly budget limit of $120 in my LAMA, which is the maximum RPS I can guarantee as operating condition?*. In fact, guiding the strategic decision of contracting external APIs and anticipating the different options of operating conditions of the system depending on the cost are critical aspects that could help software architects and DevOps of any LAMA.

These analysis questions deal with computer-aided extraction of useful information from a LAMA, which helps DevOps teams make certain decisions and detect potential issues. Trying to answer these questions even in a simple scenario leads to the conclusion that it is a tedious, time-consuming and error-prone activity. In addition, as the LAMA has some complexity, performing these analyses manually will be neither reliable nor cost-effective, and its automation would be of great value to software architects. We have coined this problem as the **problem of automated capacity analysis of LAMAs**. This capacity analysis comprises the automation of different *analysis operations* that arise from the **number of requests, the cost and the time**, which are the three essential cornerstones of this problem. This problem is novel and has not been fully explored in the literature. Existing work has always omitted at least one of the three essential dimensions of a LAMA. We think that this is because no existing proposal studies the relationship between them. The *QoS-aware service composition* problem is related to this topic, but does not fully address all the features of LAMAs, as described in Sect. 3.

In this paper, we coin the term LAMA, describe the problem of automated capacity analysis of LAMAs, and present an approach to solving it by interpreting it as an optimisation problem implementable as a constraint satisfaction and optimisation problem (CSOP). We also present an extensible catalogue of analysis operations and a public RESTful API that transforms a LAMA into an initial implementation using the MiniZinc modelling language [17] and provides solutions for basic analysis operations.

The remainder of this paper is structured as follows. In Sect. 2, we introduce and define the different concepts that serve as background. In Sect. 3, we explore related work and explain why their proposals are not useful in this situation. In Sect. 4, we provide an initial definition of this problem through a synthetic example. In Sect. 5 we present a preliminary approach and a possible model of the problem using a CSOP. In Sect. 6 we present a public RESTful API that provides solutions for three basic analysis operations. Finally, in Sect. 7 we summarise the conclusions of this paper and describe future work.

2   Background

2.1   Pricing Plans

API providers usually sell the functionality through multiple *pricing plans*, or simply *pricings* [12]. In the widely used case of RESTful APIs the functionality is defined as a set of endpoints (expressed as URLs) to resources that can be operated (with the HTTP directives). In such a context, a given API could have a number of endpoints and their specific pricing plans would specify the expected operating conditions for each endpoint. For the sake of clarity, from now on, in this paper we will assume an important simplification: each API only has a single endpoint and a single operational directive.

In the scenario depicted in Fig. 1, E1 has two plans: *Basic*, with a price of $5/month, a limitation of 15 RPS and another limitation of 1,000 requests per day (RPD); and *Premium*, for $8/month, 25 RPS and 10,000 RPD; also, E2 has two plans: *Silver*, with a price of $4/month and a limitation of 10 RPS; and *Gold*, for $10/month and 20 RPS.

Pricing plans are usually paid through subscriptions, which tend to be billed monthly or yearly. The more expensive plans have less restrictive limitations. Some plans may also include an *overage* cost, that is, they allow clients to exceed their limitations for an additional fee (e.g. $0.01 per request beyond the imposed limitation in the example of Fig. 1).

When clients subscribe to a pricing plan, they usually obtain a personal *API key* to identify their own requests and help providers apply the appropriate limitations. It is possible for a single client to obtain multiple keys for the same plan to overcome its limitations. Nonetheless, providers commonly limit the number of requests that can be sent from the same IP address to prevent a client from obtaining too many keys, especially for free plans.

2.2   Topology of a LAMA

A LAMA is an MSA with at least one external API that is regulated by a pricing plan, which includes, among other things, capacity limits and usage price.

As shown in Fig. 1, the topology of a LAMA can be represented as a DAG (directed acyclic diagram), where each dark node corresponds to an internal service in the LAMA and a light node corresponds to an external API. Each directed edge between nodes represents a consumption from one node to another: e.g. *microservice S1 consumes microservices S2 and S3, microservice S2 consumes external API E1, and microservice S3 consumes external APIs E1 and E2.* Each edge is labeled with the number of requests that are derived from the invocation of the consumer service: e.g. *each time the microservice S1 is invoked, the microservice S2 is consumed 3 times and microservice S3 is consumed 2 times.*

It is worth noting that, for simplicity, we are using a maximal consumption modelling of the LAMA, assuming that every request is always necessary, which is not always true. Sometimes, sending certain requests depends on some conditions that must be met, and this fact could be considered through statistic and probabilistic analysis. Furthermore, we assume that requests do not consume any time and are immediate.

2.3 Capacity of an MSA

In general, *capacity* of an MSA refers to the maximum workload that it can handle, although there is no widely accepted definition for the term.

In our context, we consider the capacity of an entire MSA as the capacity of a given *entrypoint*. An entrypoint is the service of the MSA that is invoked first when a customer uses it, and then sends the appropriate requests to other services, which, in turn, may send further requests to more services.

While there is no standard metric for the capacity, existing work in the literature commonly uses the number of requests per unit of time as the metric of choice. User interactions with a LAMA through a user interface translate into requests that are sent to internal service endpoints (the entrypoints). Similarly, if the LAMA offers a public API, interactions with it are done through requests to some entrypoints.

3   Related Work

We are not aware of any existing proposal which analyses the capacity of an MSA with external APIs regulated by pricing plans. The most similar proposal, which has also been a major inspiration for us, is ELeCTRA by Gamez–Diaz et al. [10]. Based on the limitations of an external API (specified in its pricing) and the topology of an MSA with a single entrypoint, ELeCTRA computes the maximum values of the limitations that the entrypoint of the MSA will be able to offer to its users. Assuming that the topology of the MSA does not vary, these maximum values are determined solely by the values of the external API limitations, i.e., they are induced by them. This analysis of the limitations induced in an MSA is performed by ELeCTRA by interpreting the problem as a CSOP and using MiniZinc [17] as a solver.

Unfortunately, ELeCTRA's capabilities are insufficient to automatically analyse the capacity of a LAMA. Its main limitation is to consider that a pricing consists of a single constraint, or a single quota or a single limit. Thus, it is not possible to model prices, overage cost, or specify several limits (quotas and rates) in the same pricing. Consequently, none of the questions (Q1-Q6) raised in Sect. 1 could be solved with ELeCTRA.

Capacity analysis of LAMAs is also closely related to the *QoS-aware composition* problem. It tackles the selection of the best *providers* for different *tasks* in an architecture, based on QoS attributes offered by these providers that need to be optimised depending on user needs. This problem can be solved using search based techniques, using either Integer Linear Programming [23] or non-deterministic approaches [3, 20]. Drawing inspiration from these proposals, we could adapt their approaches to our problem, interpreting the LAMA as a composite service where the QoS attributes of each provider correspond to the attributes of a pricing plan. Nevertheless, this interpretation presents some limitations that does not allow a complete capacity analysis of a LAMA, in particular:

- No proposal considers capacity limitations of external providers, instead focusing on other attributes such as availability or response time.
- Each attribute needs an aggregation function that is used to select the best provider for each task. No aggregation function can model the exact semantics of rates and quotas, especially considering that they are defined over different time windows.
- No proposal defines analysis operations about capacity, time windows and cost.
- In previous work, a task could only be associated with a single provider. In our approach, there may be a need to use multiple API keys from the same provider to perform the same task.
- In real-world systems, a single provider can define multiple pricing plans for the same task. These plans differ in their cost, quotas, rates and other attributes. This was not the case in the previous approach, where a provider only had one plan for a task. Additionally, a LAMA might send multiple requests to the same provider.
- There might be cases where there is no solution to the problem, e.g. the LAMA is not able to serve enough requests to meet user requirements given the subscribed pricing plans. In previous approaches, this aspect was not taken into account.

4   Capacity Analysis of LAMAs

The capacity of a LAMA refers to the maximum workload that it can handle over a given period of time and at a maximum cost, without exceeding any of the external limitations derived from subscribed pricing plans. This definition is in line with the *capacity and performance management practice* in ITILv4 [15].

The capacity analysis of a LAMA should provide answers to the software architects and DevOps to make decisions over the subscribed external APIs and the potential operating conditions for the LAMA users. In particular, this analysis should take into account three dimensions that are intertwined:

- *Metrics.* This dimension addresses the metrics (bounded to a scale) that have an impact on the capacity or are constrained by external APIs. In this paper we focus on a single metric, *number of requests*, that is the most widely used metric in the industry [11] and is constrained and limited in most commercial API pricing plans. It is important to note that the metric should always be bounded to a particular scale. In the case of *number of requests*, we could have different time scales such as Requests Per Second (RPS) or Requests Per Hour (RPH).
- *Temporality.* This dimension represents the temporal boundaries for the capacity to be analyzed. In this context, the same LAMA could have different capacities depending on the time period when it is calculated. These boundaries are typically linked with the desired operating conditions or, in case of a SaaS, the defined pricing plans. As an example, in Fig. 1, since both LAMAs pricing plans and external APIs plans are stated in terms of months, the appropriate temporal boundaries for the capacity analysis should only address a monthly perspective. However, in a more realistic setting there could be scenarios where different external APIs have different plan periods and consequently, the capacity analysis should combine multiple temporal perspectives involved.
- *Cost.* This dimension takes into account the derived costs from the infrastructure operation and the cost derived from the contracted plans with the different external APIs. In the example of Fig. 1, multiple options are possible, depending on the number of plans contracted; we assume that it is possible to contract multiple times a particular plan as this is the norm in the real API market.

For example, given the LAMA in Fig. 1, the capacity can be analysed by manual calculations. In 1 s, using the cheapest plans and no overage cost, the capacity of the LAMA is 1 RPS, because 1 request to S1 results in 8 requests to E1, and one more request to S1 would result in 16 requests to E1, thus exceeding the limitation of the *Basic* plan. The cost is a fixed value, $9 in this case. In 2 s, the maximum number of requests allowed to E1 using the *Basic* plan is 30; therefore, the capacity is 3 RPS, resulting in 24 requests to E1 and 12 to E2. The cost, however, remains the same.

When dealing with real-world architectures, the number of internal services and external APIs is considerably high, and thus there is a great number of plans and possible combinations. Additionally, when defining the pricing plans to be offered to the LAMA customers, it is fundamental to know the limitations derived from the usage by the external APIs together with its associated cost. In fact, these costs will be part of the operational costs of the LAMA, and are essential when analysing the OpEx (Operational Expenditures) [1] for the desired operating conditions in general, and to have profitable pricing plans in the case of a SaaS LAMA.

5   Automated Capacity Analysis

Automated LAMA capacity analysis deals with extracting information from the model of a LAMA using automated mechanisms. Analysing LAMA models is an error-prone and tedious task, and it is infeasible to do it manually with large-scale and complex LAMA models. In this paper we propose a similar approach to that followed in other fields, i.e., to support the analysis process from a catalogue of analysis operations (analysis of feature models [2,5], service level agreements [16,18,19] and Business Process [21]).

In this sense, all the analysis operations we have faced so far can be interpreted in terms of optimal search problems. Therefore, they can be solved through Search Based Software Engineering (SBSE) techniques, similarly to other cloud engineering problems [13]. We tackle this problem as a Constraint Satisfaction and Optimisation Problem (CSOP), where, *grosso modo*, the search space corresponds to the set of tuples (*Requests, Time, Cost*) that conform valid operating conditions of the LAMA. The objective function is defined on the variable that needs to be optimised in each case: requests, time or cost.

5.1   Formal Description of LAMAs

The primary objective of formalising a LAMA is to establish a sound basis for the automated support. Following the formalisation principles defined by Hofstede et al. [14], we follow a transformational style by translating the LAMA specification to a target domain suitable for the automated analysis (*Primary Goal Principle*). Specifically, we propose translating the specification to a CSOP that can be then analysed using state-of-the-art constraint programming tools.

A CSOP is defined as a 3-tuple (V, D, C) composed of a set of variables V, their domains D and a number of constraints C. A solution for a CSOP is an assignment of values to the variables in V from their domains in D so that all the constraints in C are satisfied.

Due to lack of space, we summarised the most relevant aspects of mapping a LAMA into a CSOP in our supplementary material [9]. The following paragraphs explain how the different elements and relationships of a LAMA are translated into a CSOP, mentioning the different variables and parameters that are needed to model the problem:

- **Positive number of requests.** All internal services and external APIs must serve a positive number of requests. Therefore, all variables $reqs_{S_i}$ and req_{E_i} that denote the request served by internal services and external APIs respectively must be greater than or equal to 0.
- **Requests served by internal services.** Each internal service in the LAMA S_i must serve all requests sent to it by every other service S_j, denoted as $reqs_{S_j S_i}$. Thus, for each internal service there is a constraint $reqs_{S_i} = \sum_{j=1}^{n} reqs_{S_j S_i} \cdot reqs_{S_j}$.

- **Requests served by external APIs.** Each external API E_i must serve all requests sent to it by the internal services S_j, denoted as $reqs_{S_j E_i}$. External APIs do not send requests between them. Thus, for each external API there is a constraint $req_{E_i} = \sum_{j=1}^{n} reqs_{S_j E_i} \cdot reqs_{S_j}$. Additionally, the total number of served requests is the sum of the requests sent to each plan below its limitations, $limReq_{ij}$, and the requests sent over the limitations, $ovgReq_{ij}$. This differentiation in two variables helps us obtain the number of overage requests more easily. Thus, for each plan P_{ij} of external API E_i there is a constraint $req_{E_i} = \sum_{j=1}^{n} limReq_{ij} + ovgReq_{ij}$. Furthermore, no requests can be sent using a plan with no keys, so for each plan there is a constraint $limReq_{ij} > 0 \rightarrow keys_{ij} > 0$. Also, no overage requests can be sent if there are no requests below limitations, so for each plan there is another constraint $ovgReq_{ij} > 0 \rightarrow limReq_{ij} > 0$.
- **Quota of each pricing plan.** The number of requests served by each external API E_i must not exceed any quota q_{ij}, defined over a time unit qu_{ij}. Multiple keys $keys_{ij}$ for each plan may be obtained. For each external API E_i and each of its respective plans P_{ij}, there is a constraint $limReq_{ij} <= keys_{ij} \cdot q_{ij} \cdot \lceil time/qu_{ij} \rceil$.
- **Rate of each pricing plan.** The number of requests served by each external API E_i must not exceed any rate r_{ij}, defined over a time unit ru_{ij}. Note that rates need to account for the time unit of the quota, as the rate is reset at the beginning of each unit. Therefore, for each external API E_i and each of its respective plans P_{ij}, there is a constraint $limReq_{ij} - qu_{ij} \cdot \lfloor time/qu_{ij} \rfloor <= keys_{ij} \cdot r_{ij} \cdot \lceil time \bmod qu_{ij}/ru_{ij} \rceil$. If a plan has no no quota, the constraint is simplified to $limReq_i <= keys_{ij} \cdot r_{ij} \cdot \lceil time/ru_{ij} \rceil$.
- **OpEx of each external API.** The cost of each external API E_i is the sum of the subscriptions to each plan P_{ij} plus overage costs. For each external API E_i, there is a constraint $OpEx_i = \sum_{j=1}^{n} keys_{ij} \cdot cost_{ij} + ovg_{ij} \cdot ovgReq_{ij}$.
- **Total OpEx.** The total cost of the LAMA is the sum of the cost of each external API. There is a constraint $OpEx = \sum_{i=1}^{n} OpEx_i$.

5.2 Analysis Operations

We propose a catalogue of three analysis operations that leverage the formal description of LAMAs to automatically extract helpful information. Analogous analysis operations have been defined in the context of the automated analysis of feature models [2], service level agreements [16,18,19] and in the area of MSAs [10] (we may remark that it is not our intention to propose an exhaustive set of analysis operations as that would exceed the scope of this paper). For the description of the operations as CSOPs, we will refer to the input specification of a LAMA L and a variable v. Additionally, we will use the following auxiliary operations:

- `map(L)`. This operation translates a LAMA specification L to a CSP following the mapping described in Sect. 5.1 and more detailed in [9].

- `minimize(CSP, v)`. This standard CSOP-based operation returns a solution for the input `CSP` (if any) with the minimum value of variable `v`.
- `maximize(CSP, v)`. Same that prior operation but with the maximum value of variable `v`.

In what follows, we present three basic analysis operations, and, for the first operations identified in Sect. 1, we provide an explanation of how it is mapped to a CSOP from the corresponding basic operation.

Maximum Number of Requests. This operation returns the maximum number of requests that a LAMA L is able to serve, over a specific time window t and for a maximum total cost c. This operation can be translated to a CSOP as follows:

$$\text{maxRequests}(L, t, c) \iff \text{maximize}(\text{map}(L) \wedge \text{time} = t \wedge \text{OpEx} <= c, \text{reqL})$$

With this operation we can answer question Q2 (*Assuming we have a Basic plan and a Gold plan already contracted what is the maximal RPM I can guarantee to all my 20 customers?*) in Sect. 1 resulting in 5.6 RPS to each customer:

$$\text{Q2} \iff \text{maxRequests}(L, 60\,\text{s}, 15)/20 = 5.6 \text{ req}$$

Similarly, question Q3 (*Assuming we have a monthly budget limit of \$120 in my LAMA, which is the maximum RPS to each of 20 customers?*) is translated into maxRequests(L, 1s, 120)/20, resulting in 1.35 (that is, 1) RPS to each customer:

$$\text{Q3} \iff \text{maxRequests}(L, 1\,\text{s}, 120)/20 = 1.35 \text{ req}$$

Minimum Cost. This operation returns the minimum cost of the LAMA L, so that it can serve a minimum of RL requests over a time window t. From the result of this operation we can obtain the optimum (cheapest) plan combination (including the number of keys to be subscribed for each plan and possible overage requests). The translation of this operation to a CSOP is as follows:

$$\text{minCost}(L, RL, t) \iff \text{minimize}(\text{map}(L) \wedge \text{reqL} = RL \wedge \text{time} = t, \text{OpEx})$$

The question Q1 (*What is the cheapest operational cost for my LAMA in order to offer 2 RPS to 20 customers?*) is translated into minCost(L, 2 · 20, 1s), resulting in a total cost of \$174:

$$\text{Q1} \iff \text{minCost}(L, 2 \cdot 20, 1\,\text{s}) = \$174$$

Minimum Time. This operation returns the minimum time that a LAMA L needs to serve at least RL requests, given a maximum total cost c. This operation can be translated to a CSOP as follows:

$$\text{minTime}(L, RL, c) \iff \text{minimize}(\text{map}(L) \wedge \text{reqL} = RL \wedge \text{OpEx} <= c, \text{time})$$

6   Validation

In order to verify that our proposal can be exploited in a useful way, we have developed a tooling support that partially supports it. Specifically, we have developed a RESTful API that provides our 3 basic capacity analysis operations, and a deepnote notebook that shows the Python implementation of the 6 analysis questions posed in Sect. 1. This tooling support can and should be understood as a minimal but solid proof of concept.

Smart LAMA [8],[1] is a public RESTful API that supports, among others, various endpoints which transform a LAMA into a CSOP using the MiniZinc modelling language. In particular, for the scope of this paper, we will focus on the three main endpoints that provide solutions to the three analysis operations described in the previous section.

All endpoints start with the base URL `/api/v2/operations`. They support the POST method and require the formal description of the LAMA to be included in the request body. The response includes the result of the operation (a number) and the MiniZinc output (a string containing the final values of all variables used to solve the CSOP).

- `/maxRequests`. This operation returns the maximum number of requests that the LAMA is able to serve per unit of time without exceeding any external limitation. It supports some query parameters: `OpEx` is used to specify a maximum total budget that can be spent to subscribe to the different pricing plans; `time` can be used to specify the unit of time in which the operation is calculated (indicated as the number of seconds, e.g. a minute is represented as 60); and `K-<API>-<Plan>` is used to indicate a specific number of subscriptions to a plan (e.g. `K-E1-Basic=1` means that there is 1 subscription to plan *Basic* of API E1). Note that there will be no restriction to the total cost of the LAMA if no OpEx or specific subscriptions are indicated.
- `/minCost`. This operation returns the minimum cost to serve a certain number of requests, which is specified using the `reqL` query parameter, over a certain time window, specified through the `time` query parameter. Both parameters are required. Obtaining the minimum cost implies obtaining the optimum combination of subscriptions to the pricing plans, which is also included within the MiniZinc output and may be extracted if needed.
- `/minTime`. This operation returns the minimum time (in number of seconds) in which the LAMA can serve a certain number of requests, which is specified using the `reqL` query parameter. This endpoint also supports the `OpEx` and `K-<API>-<Plan>` parameters, which work exactly as described above.

The formal description of a LAMA used in the notebook is a JSON-based language which we named *LAMA-DL*. Due to lack of space, we will not explain how to transform a LAMA into LAMA-DL. Nonetheless, we believe that the example included in the notebook using the LAMA in Fig. 1 is self-explanatory and contains all supported elements.

---

[1] Available at https://smart-lama-api-beta.herokuapp.com/api/v2.

Note that, by default, the API is set up to assume that no overage requests should be used. To enable the use of overage requests, all operations support the `useOvg` query parameter, which should be explicitly set to `true`. Only pricing plans with overage costs may have overage requests.

A known issue of the transformation into a MiniZinc model is that it generates a considerable amount of internal variables that, in some situations, may have very high values and cause *out of bounds* errors. To minimise these errors, we decided to limit the maximum number of subscriptions to each plan to 10. This workaround has proven to be useful based on our own experience. Furthermore, it is very uncommon to obtain that many subscriptions to a single plan, as API providers usually have limitations on the number of subscriptions per client or IP address.

To validate Smart LAMA, we developed an online Deepnote notebook [7]. It contains wrappers that take a formal description of a LAMA as input, send the appropriate request to the API using the corresponding query parameters, and return the solution provided by MiniZinc, including the final values of all internal variables after solving the CSOP. The notebook includes a complete example based on the LAMA in Fig. 1 and shows how to use the API to solve each of the 6 different analysis questions introduced in Sect. 1. Note that the notebook has *Execute* access, meaning that its cells can be executed but not edited. However, it can be duplicated and then edited.

Some examples of API calls included in the notebook [7] are the following:

- **Q1. What is the cheapest operational cost for my LAMA in order to offer 2 RPS to 20 customers?** In this operation, the total number of requests that the LAMA should serve is $2 \cdot 20 = 40$. This operation can be solved using the endpoint `/api/v2/operations/minCost?reqL=40&time=1`.
- **Q5. Assuming we have a Basic plan and a Gold plan already contracted what is the maximal RPS I can guarantee as operating condition?** Using the endpoint `/api/v2/operations/maxRequests?K-E1-Basic=1&K-E1-Premium=0&K-E2-Silver=0&K-E2-Gold=1&time=1` it is possible to obtain the solution to this operation. Note that we are assuming that we do not want any additional subscriptions besides one *Basic* and one *Gold*. Therefore, the number of subscriptions to *Premium* and *Silver* must be set to 0. Otherwise, there would be no limitation to the number of subscriptions to these two plans.
- **Q6. Assuming we have a monthly budget limit of $120 in my LAMA, which is the maximum RPS I can guarantee as operating condition?.** The endpoint `/api/v2/operations/maxRequests?OpEx=120&time=1` provides a solution to this operation.

7   Conclusions and Future Work

In this paper, we presented the problem of automating the capacity analysis of microservices architectures in situations where the MSA consumes external APIs that define pricing plans. We introduced the concept of *limitation-aware microservices architecture* (LAMA) and explored the different dimensions involved in the capacity analysis of a LAMA. We listed 6 analysis questions, which we determined to be derived from three basic analysis operations that allow the definition of any number of other operations. We presented a public API that transforms a LAMA into a proof-of-concept implementation of these operations using MiniZinc, and evaluated it in a synthetic LAMA example. We are confident that our proposal will prove useful to DevOps teams who need to deal with issues related to capacity analysis of LAMAs.

We are aware that our tooling support is partial and therefore incomplete, but it shows the real possibility of answering questions in less time than if it were done manually. In this sense, we are working on using notation to describe both the topology and the pricing closer to some of the available technology.

Furthermore, as future work, we would like to improve and extend our proposal in order to support more complex operations. We want to consider the addition of limitations in internal services, which usually have restrictions from their deployment infrastructures. Additionally, we need to support multiple entrypoints, as it is uncommon for LAMAs to only have a single operation.

Acknowledgments. Grants   RTI2018-101204-B-C21, RTI2018-101204-B-C22, PID2021-126227NB-C21, PID2021-126227NB-C22 funded by MCIN/AEI/10.13039/501100011033/ and "ERDF a way of making Europe"; grants P18-FR-2895, US-1264651 and US-1381595 funded by Junta de Andalucia /ERDF, UE; and grant FPU19/00666 funded by MCIN/AEI/ 10.13039/501100011033 and by "ESF Investing in your future".

References

1. Andreo, S., Calà, A., Bosch, J.: OpEx driven software architecture a case study. In: Proceedings of the 15th European Conference on Software Architecture (ECSA) (Companion) (2021)
2. Benavides, D., Segura, S., Ruiz-Cortés, A.: Automated analysis of feature models 20 years later: a literature review. Inf. Syst. **35**(6), 615–636 (2010)
3. Canfora, G., Di Penta, M., Esposito, R., Villani, M.L.: A lightweight approach for QoS-aware service composition. In: Proceedings of the 2nd International Conference on Service Oriented Computing (ICSOC 2004)-short papers. Citeseer (2004)
4. How to build an API economy for your enterprise - Capgemini. https://www.capgemini.com/2020/12/how-to-build-an-api-economy-for-your-enterprise/. Accessed 13 June 2022
5. Durán, A., Benavides, D., Segura, S., Trinidad, P., Ruiz-Cortés, A.: Flame: a formal framework for the automated analysis of software product lines validated by automated specification testing. Softw. Syst. Model. **16**(4), 1049–1082 (2017)
6. Fowler, M.: Microservices. https://martinfowler.com/articles/microservices.html. Accessed 13 June 2022
7. Fresno-Aranda, R., Fernández, P., Durán, A., Ruiz-Cortés, A.: Notebook for automated analysis of a basic LAMA. https://bit.ly/smart-lama-api
8. Fresno-Aranda, R., Fernández, P., Ruiz-Cortés, A.: Smart LAMA API: automated capacity analysis of limitation-aware microservices architectures. In: Proceedings of the XVII Jornadas de Ingeniería de Ciencia e Ingeniería de Servicios (In press). SISTEDES (2022)

9. Fresno-Aranda, R., Fernández, P., Durán, A., Ruiz-Cortés, A.: Semi-Automated Capacity Analysis of Limitation- Aware Microservices Architectures (Supplementary Material) (2022). https://doi.org/10.5281/zenodo.7025641
10. Gamez-Diaz, A., Fernandez, P., Pautasso, C., Ivanchikj, A., Ruiz-Cortes, A.: ELeCTRA: induced usage limitations calculation in RESTful APIs. In: Liu, X., et al. (eds.) ICSOC 2018. LNCS, vol. 11434, pp. 435–438. Springer, Cham (2019). https://doi.org/10.1007/978-3-030-17642-6_39
11. Gamez-Diaz, A., Fernandez, P., Ruiz-Cortes, A.: An analysis of RESTful APIs offerings in the industry. In: Maximilien, M., Vallecillo, A., Wang, J., Oriol, M. (eds.) ICSOC 2017. LNCS, vol. 10601, pp. 589–604. Springer, Cham (2017). https://doi.org/10.1007/978-3-319-69035-3_43
12. Gamez-Diaz, A., et al.: The role of limitations and SLAs in the API industry. In: Proceedings of the 27th ACM Joint Meeting on European Software Engineering Conference and Symposium on the Foundations of Software Engineering (ESEC/FSE), pp. 1006–1014 (2019)
13. Harman, M., Lakhotia, K., Singer, J., White, D.R., Yoo, S.: Cloud engineering is search based software engineering too. J. Syst. Softw. 86(9), 2225–2241 (2013)
14. ter Hofstede, A.H., Proper, H.A.: How to formalize it?: formalization principles for information system development methods. Inf. Softw. Technol. 40(10), 519–540 (1998)
15. ITIL Capacity Management. https://www.smartsheet.com/content/itil-capacity-management. Accessed 13 June 2022
16. Martín-Díaz, O., Ruiz-Cortés, A., Durán, A., Müller, C.: An approach to temporal-aware procurement of web services. In: Benatallah, B., Casati, F., Traverso, P. (eds.) ICSOC 2005. LNCS, vol. 3826, pp. 170–184. Springer, Heidelberg (2005). https://doi.org/10.1007/11596141_14
17. MiniZinc constraint modeling language. https://www.minizinc.org/. Accessed 13 June 2022
18. Müller, C., Gutierrez, A.M., Fernandez, P., Martín-Díaz, O., Resinas, M., Ruiz-Cortés, A.: Automated validation of compensable SLAs. IEEE Trans. Serv. Comput. 14(5), 1306–1319 (2018)
19. Müller, C., Resinas, M., Ruiz-Cortés, A.: Automated analysis of conflicts in WS-Agreement. IEEE Trans. Serv. Comput. 7(4), 530–544 (2013)
20. Parejo, J.A., Segura, S., Fernandez, P., Ruiz-Cortés, A.: QoS-Aware web services composition using GRASP with path relinking. Exp. Syst. Appl. 41(9), 4211–4223 (2014)
21. del Río-Ortega, A., Resinas, M., Cabanillas, C., Ruiz-Cortés, A.: On the definition and design-time analysis of process performance indicators. Inf. Syst. 38(4), 470–490 (2013)
22. How to Make the API Economy a Reality - WSO2. https://wso2.com/choreo/resources/how-to-make-the-api-economy-a-reality/. Accessed 13 June 2022
23. Zeng, L., Benatallah, B., Ngu, A.H., Dumas, M., Kalagnanam, J., Chang, H.: QoS-aware middleware for web services composition. IEEE Trans. Soft. Eng. 30(5), 311–327 (2004)

Edge-to-Cloud Solutions for Self-adaptive Machine Learning-Based IoT Applications
A Cost Comparison

Marco Emilio Poleggi[✉], Nabil Abdennadher, Raoul Dupuis,
and Francisco Mendonça

ISC Department, University of Applied Sciences and Arts, Western Switzerland,
Geneva, Switzerland
{marco-emilio.poleggi,nabil.abdennadher,raoul.dupuis,
francisco.mendonca}@hesge.ch

Abstract. Large-scale IoT applications based on machine learning (ML) demand both edge and cloud processing for, respectively, AI inference and ML training tasks. Context-aware applications also need self-adaptive intelligence which makes their architecture even more complex. Estimating the costs of operating such edge-to-cloud deployments is challenging. To this purpose, we propose a reference service-oriented event-driven system architecture for IoT/edge applications comprising a minimal set of components, mapped on available cloud services. We then propose a resource consumption model for estimating the cost of deploying and running self-adaptive AI-assisted IoT applications on selected edge-to-cloud platforms. The model is evaluated in two scenarios: Road Traffic Management and Smart Grid. We finally provide some estimates showing how the expenditure breakdown varies significantly depending on the adopted platform: storage costs are dominant in Road Traffic Management for all providers, whereas either messaging or edge management costs may dominate the Smart Grid scenario, and, surprisingly, computing costs are almost negligible in all cases.

Keywords: Edge · Cloud · IoT · Cost Model · PaaS

1 Introduction

Nowadays, the Cloud is being massively adopted for a plethora of applications, many of which also need some components deployed at the Edge, in charge of governing large-scale IoT sensor networks: we refer to these as *edge-to-cloud* IoT deployments. A particular subclass of these IoT applications is based on machine learning (ML) to accomplish inference tasks on data coming from IoT sensors: traffic monitoring systems, environmental sensing, fleet management and asset tracking, as well as smart grid appliances. Because of their distributed nature over edge devices with constrained resources, these applications leverage the Cloud for (heavy, long-term) learning tasks, while exploiting edge devices for (light, low-latency) inference tasks on data coming from nearby IoT sensors.

© The Author(s), under exclusive license to Springer Nature Switzerland AG 2023
J. Á. Bañares et al. (Eds.): GECON 2022, LNCS 13430, pp. 89–102, 2023.
https://doi.org/10.1007/978-3-031-29315-3_8

Many IoT applications also exhibit high context sensitivity, as their intelligence has to cope with different physical settings, complex usage patterns as well as varying meteorological conditions. All this demand "context-aware" solutions, which, for optimized performance, would follow a "self-adaptive" paradigm, as illustrated in Fig. 1: an end-user application consumes the output of an edge device that processes data coming from some IoT sensors. An artificial intelligence-based (AI) inference module is deployed on this edge device, which makes "predictions" on the sensing data: e.g., classify environmental sounds, recognize car license plates, etc. The AI inference module is endowed with a machine learning model (MLM) specifically tailored to the application at hand and optimized for the edge device. This MLM is built and trained in the Cloud, where an AI learning module is deployed.

Such applications operate in the following way. During a bootstrap phase, a raw dataset is fed to the Cloud where it is first labeled and then processed for AI learning. That results in a first MLM which is deployed to the edge device. Then, the system enters operation mode: a feedback loop enabling continuous intelligence adaptation. The edge device autonomously processes IoT sensors' data; two cases may occur:

a. The prediction is satisfying: application output is provided.
b. The prediction is not satisfying: no application output is provided; the related sensing input is uploaded to the Cloud as "low-performance" data. These are labeled and fed for training to the AI learning module: a new MLM is generated which is then redeployed to the edge device. The original dataset is extended with the new labeled data.

Several commercial actors already offer edge-to-cloud solutions (platforms) suitable for our scenario. Given the complexity of such three-tiered (IoT, Edge and Cloud) architectures, estimating their operating costs is not trivial. In a previous work of ours [3], we presented a cloud application placement tool: a decision-support system that optimally selects a cloud provider for an application, based on current prices fed to a resource consumption model (RCM). With this paper, we go beyond the *pure* cloud application paradigm and provide a comparative study of edge-to-cloud platforms for self-adaptive machine learning-based IoT applications. Indeed, we are interested in answering the specific question: *how much does it cost to deploy and operate a generic ML-based IoT application on a given platform?*

For comparison purposes, we consider five platforms: three well-known that employ proprietary solutions (Amazon AWS [1], Google Cloud [4] and Microsoft Azure [8]) and two newcomers that are based on (mostly) open-source software (SixSq Nuvla [11] and Balena [2]).

The rest of the paper is structured as follows. We review some related work in Sect. 2. A detailed description of our use case is provided in Sect. 3 where a reference system architecture is also proposed. Then, Sect. 4 presents our RCM based on which we compare the cost of the different edge-to-cloud solutions under study (Sect. 5). Finally, we draw our conclusions in Sect. 6.

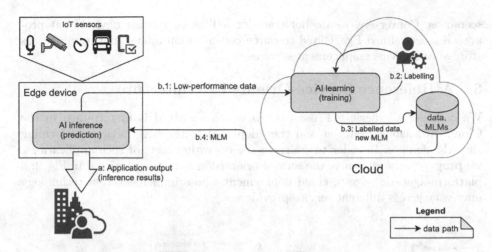

Fig. 1. A self-adaptive ML-based edge-to-cloud application scenario (operation feedback loop).

2   Related Work

Several research works aim to estimate the placement or operating costs of end-user applications on different cloud service providers. To the best of our knowledge, none has yet proposed an all-comprehensive cost model for complex IoT applications.

Martens et al. [7] tackle the case of customers who own their IT infrastructure and want to compare public cloud offerings. They propose a mathematical method to compute the Total Cost of Ownership (TCO) of cloud computing services. This work set the basis for our previous RCM [3], which is extended here to especially deal with ML-based IoT/edge applications.

Laatikainen et al. [6] study the different pricing models of many IaaS, PaaS, and SaaS cloud providers. They realize that, despite the heterogeneity and complexity of the models, common offering patterns exist, however no established normalized price strategy is available. Thus, the authors propose an extended SBIFT-based pricing model customized for generic cloud services.

Nguyen et al. [9] study the optimal placement of IoT/edge applications in cloud systems employing virtual network functions. Based on a system architecture with focus on the IoT network topology, they define an analytical cost model in terms of computation resources and network bandwidth, as well as algorithms for small and large-scale network settings. Our analysis is instead focused to the cost of edge-to-cloud service architectures.

With the goal of simulating an infrastructure-agnostic IoT/fog application placement method, Goudarzi et al. [5] propose a novel Memetic algorithm which minimizes the operating costs in terms of execution time and energy consumption. Local IoT computation is compared to both Edge and Cloud offloading scenarios. Conversely, we do not consider IoT as computing devices, but propose a more refined Ege/Cloud resource consumption model that encompasses storage and device management services.

3   A Reference Service-Oriented Architecture

We consider a generic IoT use case in which an MLM is first trained in the Cloud on a labeled dataset and then deployed to the edge devices performing the AI inference. In order to estimate the operating costs of such applications, we propose, as a reference, the service-oriented architecture depicted in Fig. 2: a platform-agnostic edge-to-cloud deployment whose implementation technology may vary across different service providers.

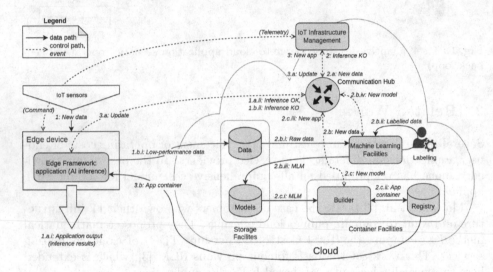

Fig. 2. Reference architecture for a generic self-adaptive ML-based IoT application (edge-to-cloud deployment). Event labels are numbered according to the application workflow described below.

The minimal set of necessary service components is:

IoT Infrastructure Management to compose, provision and monitor Edge/IoT networks. Edge devices and their companion IoT devices are mostly autonomous; their Edge Framework modules are packaged into some form and provisioned to them from a Cloud repository. As a best practice, a dedicated control path would be used for IoT Infrastructure Management operations–especially for monitoring and telemetry tasks.

Edge Framework to enable edge modules programming and execution as micro services. We assume that Edge Framework artifacts (OS and application modules) are provisioned as Docker containers–possibly the most popular way of deploying micro services without resorting to provider-specific services like those based on Functions-as-a-Service (FaaS).

Container Facilities to build a Docker container with a trained MLM and possibly other Edge Framework artifacts, and to store it in a Cloud registry. Edge devices would then pull containers directly from the registry. A full-fledged *builder* component would enable automatic (event-driven) (re)building of containers.

Communication Hub to create an event-based messaging service among the different application's modules: the reception of an event triggers a workflow operation.

Storage Facilities to store labeled training data and several MLM versions in Cloud data warehouses.

Machine Learning Facilities: to build and train a MLM in the Cloud. In the case of a supervised learning strategy, we assume that the associated labeling task is performed by humans.

The service-oriented architecture depicted in Fig. 2 is event-based and data-driven. Once the system bootstrap phase has been performed, the application workflow follows the logic described in Algorithm 1 (Edge) and Algorithm 2 (Cloud).

See [10] for a detailed discussion of how the different platforms cover the above components, and how their respective service-level offerings compare to each other.

4 Resource Consumption Model

In order to estimate the operating cost of a self-adaptive ML-based IoT application, we need to further specify the edge application. We are interested in large-scale scenarios characterized by different and varying operating conditions that cannot be tackled with a unique, static MLM configuration. Thus, we need an edge AI that is 1. tailored to different contexts by leveraging several MLMs (context-awareness), and 2. continuously improved over time through recurrent retraining of its MLMs (self-adaptation). For the sake of clarity, we consider two example scenarios: Road Traffic Management and Smart Grid. In the former case, camera-less sound sensors perform vehicle classification according to the noise they generate; this application is context-aware since the noise generated by a vehicle depends on several aspects: wet/dry weather, pavement type, street configuration, surroundings, etc. In the latter case, edge devices are deployed in households to predict electrical energy consumption and production; this application is context-aware because the prediction depends on different settings: urban/rural, season, weather, weekdays/weekend, etc.

Algorithm 1: Edge Processing

```
     task Application:
        │  Data: infThreshold
        │  forever do
  1.    │     │  newData ← edge.IoTSensor.read()
        │     │  (appResult, confidence) ← edge.AI.doInference(newData)
        │     │  if confidence > infThreshold then
        │     │     │  // The inference is satisfying
1.a.i   │     │     │  edge.sendUserOutput(appResult)
1.a.ii  │     │     │  edge.event.send('Inference_OK')
        │     │  else
        │     │     │  // The inference is *not* satisfying
1.b.i   │     │     │  edge.cloudStorage.put(newData)
1.b.ii  │     │     └  edge.event.send('Inference_KO')

     task Provisioning:
        │  // Triggered by 'Update' events (3.a.) from the Cloud Processing
        │     Algorithm 2
  3.b.  │  newAppContainer ← edge.cloudStorage.get()
        └  edge.AI.doUpdate(newAppContainer)
```

From an IoT perspective, groups (or clusters) of sensors are expected to belong to different spatio-temporal contexts, each needing its own MLM configuration. A context is defined in terms of some features, such as location, time of the day, season, weather conditions, surroundings, etc.–anything that may affect the MLM performance. Our scenarios are based on the following assumptions:

- Each context has exactly one specialized MLM–this is the simplest configuration.
- Each sensor belongs to one context at any time, but can *shift* from one context to another over time. Sensors belonging to the same context are expected to exhibit a similar behavior. We deal with context shift by simulating periodical retraining of a fixed fraction of the MLMs.
- Each sensor is connected to only one edge device to which it reports measurement events. Any edge device support as many MLMs as are the contexts of the sensors connected to it. When receiving an event from a given sensor, the corresponding MLM is triggered in the edge device, as explained in Fig. 1.

The model considers the fees for registering the edge devices and is composed of sub-models for, respectively, exchanged control messages (application and telemetry, excluding data), storage (data at rest and operations), data transfers (network usage for data moving between the Edge and the Cloud) and computing. The model's parameters are listed in Table 1: the actual values depend on the application; they are detailed in [10]. For each sub-model, we compute the application demand (workload) for one edge device. Then, for each platform under study, we chose the service resources (storage, messaging, computing, etc.) that satisfy the demand at the cheapest offering, so as to obtain a normalized price list. Based on these prices, we compute the cost of using the chosen resources on a large-scale deployment.

Algorithm 2: Cloud Processing

```
       Data: maxNewDataCount
       forever do
           newEvent ← cloud.event.receive()
           switch newEvent do
 2.        │   case 'Inference_KO' do
           │   │   // In IoT Infrastructure Managament
 2.a.      │   │   cloud.event.send('New_Data')
           │   │   cloud.dataSet.newDataCount += 1
           │   case 'New_Data' do
           │   │   // In Machine Learning Facilities
 2.b.      │   │   if cloud.dataSet.newDataCount ≥ maxNewDataCount then
 2.b.i     │   │   │   rawDataBatch ← cloud.cloudStorage.get()
 2.b.ii    │   │   │   labeledDataBatch ← cloud.labelling(rawDataBatch)
 2.b.iii   │   │   │   newMLM ← cloud.MLTraining(labeledDataBatch)
 2.b.iv    │   │   └   cloud.cloudStorage.put(newMLM)
           │   case 'New_Model' do
           │   │   // In Container Facilities
 2.c.i     │   │   newMLM ← cloud.cloudStorage.get()
 2.c.ii    │   │   newAppContainer ← cloud.containerBuilder(newMLM)
           │   │   cloud.containerRegistry.put(newAppContainer)
 2.c.iii   │   │   cloud.event.send('New_App')
 3.        │   case 'New_App' do
           │   │   // In IoT Infrastructure Management, triggers Edge's
           │   │       'Provisioning' task in Algorithm 1
 3.a.      │   └   cloud.event.send(Update')
```

With reference to Fig. 2, the edge intelligence workflow is simulated as follows:

1. **Bootstrap.** Sensors are clustered on a given feature set, resulting in a set of MLMs (`ml_contexts`). The corresponding MLMs are provisioned to the edge devices. The costs associated with the bootstrap phase are not considered because they are negligible ($<1\%$) compared to those of the operation phase.
2. **Operation.** The sensor network is started: the process is now event-driven. At a frequency of `event_rate`, each edge device is fed a "raw" sensing data item, each of size `raw_data_size`, and outputs one "application" data item, each of size `app_output_size`.
   a. **ML inference.** Inference operations are unsuccessful with probability `ml_error_rate`. Accordingly, a certain amount of raw data (in addition to the application data) is uploaded to the Cloud and stored there.
   b. **Continuous learning.** MLMs whose prediction scores fall persistently below a given threshold (which we do not specify) are said "nonperforming": they are a fraction `ml_underperf` of the total. We assume that the related MLM is retrained in the Cloud at frequency `ml_train_rate`.

Table 1. Cost model's parameters.

Parameter	Description
event_rate	Rate at which the MLM is triggered
raw_data_size	Size of a raw data item fed to the MLM
app_output_size	Size of an application output item produced by the MLM
ml_error_rate	Fraction of events which the MLM is unable to classify or predict
ml_model_size	Size of the MLM
ml_contexts	Number of contexts: each context needs a specific MLM
ml_point_size	Size of a data point used to train the MLM
ml_train_size	Number of data points used to train the MLM
ml_train_time	Computing time needed for training the MLM on 1 vCPU
ml_train_rate	Rate of MLM training rounds in the Cloud
ml_underperf	Fraction (i.e., the"nonperforming") of all MLMs that must be retrained at each round
ml_train_deadline	Maximum allowed time to train all nonperforming MLMs at each round. This sets the minimal number of needed computation resources.
edge_img_size	Size of the system package (OS, containers, MLM and libraries) deployed to any edge device
daily_connect_time	Number of minutes per day during which an edge device is connected to the Cloud
deployment_size	Number of edge devices deployed
tmetry_metrics	Number of telemetry metrics collected at the edge devices
tmetry_msg_rate	Rate at which telemetry messages are sent form the edge application to the Cloud
tmetry_msg_size	Size of a telemetry message

4.1   Messaging Model

As noted above, a well-designed edge application would use separate channels for application messages and infrastructure control messages. Hence, we consider two classes of messages: application and telemetry (which includes monitoring and logging) that are respectively handled by two different services. Notice that network usage for data transfers is excluded here.

Application messages are routed through the Communication Hub component. Telemetry messages may be conveyed through a dedicated service subcomponent of the IoT Infrastructure Management, where available; else the same Communication Hub is used. Application messages are exchanged for any operations that have to be performed in the Cloud.

4.2 Storage Operation Model

We consider the used space (data at rest) and the rate of operations performed in the Cloud storage service. Here we only attempt a rough estimate of the workload–a detailed analysis is beyond the scope of this paper. We assume that:

- Application data are uploaded to the Cloud for each MLM execution. Moreover, raw data are uploaded to the Cloud on each unsuccessful inference.
- Each upload of raw and application data to the Cloud triggers one write-like operation.
- To generate a new MLM, a set of data points, each of size `ml_point_size`, is
  1. first, transferred (read-like) from Cloud storage to the Machine Learning facilities service for labeling,
  2. then, transferred (write-like) from the Machine Learning facilities service back to Cloud storage,
  3. again, transferred (read-like) from Cloud storage to the Machine Learning facilities for training,
  4. finally, stored (write-like) for later usage (retraining).

4.3 Data Transfer Model

Data transfers may incur costs related to network usage metering, excluding application messages and telemetry. We make the following assumptions:

- Any edge device is provisioned once at bootstrap with a payload of `edge_img_size` (OS) and `ml_model_size` (MLM).
- Application output data (i.e., inference results) are always uploaded to the Cloud. Raw data are uploaded to the cloud only upon failed inference.
- We assume that the average number of learning algorithm executions is set by `ml_train_rate`. Accordingly, any affected edge device is re-provisioned with a payload of `ml_model_size + edge_img_size`.

4.4 Computing Model

When the prediction fails at the Edge, some raw (low-performance) data are uploaded to the Cloud, with the following assumptions:

- Data labeling time is not taken into account.
- If a platform does not provide an optimized ML training service, we use the pricing figures for computing resources based on equivalent or similar technology.

Our computing model:

1. Sets a target maximum training time for the whole deployment (`ml_train_deadline`), irrespective of its size and of the number of contexts.
2. Computes the sequential virtual CPU (vCPU) time (`monthly_cloud_computing_rate`) needed to train one MLM.
3. Computes the minimum number of vCPUs (`cloud_computing_vcpus`) needed to meet the training deadline for one MLM, assuming that all vCPUs run in parallel and are fully utilized, and that the training process is embarrassingly parallel.

4.5   PaaS Pricing

Edge-to-cloud platforms may charge for their services on either a pay-as-you-go or a long-term commitment basis, possibly with discounts. We consider here only platform-as-a-service (PaaS) hosting costs for long-term (1 year), large-scale deployment (1K active devices). Costs are incurred at six different service layers:

- **Edge** device management. It may incur the following costs:
  - A yearly **Subscription**.
  - A **Registered** edge device with any associated fixed costs, such as specific telemetry metrics.
  - A minute of **Connectivity**, assuming that any device is connected 24/7.
- **Messaging**. We only consider edge-cloud communication.
  - A **Telemetry** message exchanged with the Cloud.
  - An exchanged **Application** message (irrespective of its type) and any subsequent operation triggered in the Cloud: we assume that each message triggers exactly one device status update plus another Cloud operation (statistic aggregation, dashboard visualization, etc.). For platforms metering by volume, we do the appropriate conversion.
- **Data transfer**: each byte transferred from the Edge to the Cloud and vice versa, as well as between different Cloud services may incur a cost. Thus, we break this down into: **Cloud-to-Edge**, **Edge-to-Cloud** and **Intra-Cloud**. For this latter, we assume that all transfers occur within the same "availability" zone, that is, roughly speaking inside the same data center.
- **Storage**: each unit of **Space** stored incurs a cost; each **Read** and **Write** operation may incur a cost.
- **Computing**: each hour spent by any application's Cloud component incurs a cost. Additional costs for a minimum amount of attached storage are also considered.
- Technical support: **Helpdesk**.

Details about the pricing that accommodates the two scenarios for the different platforms are available elsewhere [10].

5   Operating Cost Comparison

The cost estimates are made with the assumption that each "solution" covers all the edge application's needs in terms of messaging, data transfer, storage and computation. The only fully-integrated solutions considered in this work are AWS and Azure, whereas the others need partnering with foreign service providers: we consider official partnerships when they exist, and otherwise the cheapest foreign Cloud option fulfilling the mission; foreign partnership is supposed to incur the extra provider's helpdesk costs. Specifically:

- Google Cloud does not provide native Edge infrastructure management services.
- Google has partnered with Balena, hence the complete solution "Google Cloud + Balena".
- SixSq Nuvla does not provide native telemetry, event, storage and computing services. SixSq has partnered with Exoscale for storage and computing services. The cheapest telemetry and event services are provided by AWS. Hence the complete solution "SixSq Nuvla + Exoscale + AWS".
- Balena can be used as a stand-alone Edge management platform, though it needs extra services exactly as for Nuvla. Hence the complete solution "Balena + Exoscale + AWS".
- Since AWS support fees are proportional to the total AWS charges, and AWS telemetry/event service fees account for ~28% of the whole AWS solution, the same corresponding extra hepldesk cost has to be charged to both SixSq Nuvla and Balena.

Estimates are provided for two scenarios: Road Traffic Management and Smart Grid. The values of the cost model's parameters (c.f. Table 1) of these two scenarios are detailed in [10].

Scenario: Road Traffic Management. In this scenario, the edge devices classify transiting vehicles by sampling environment noise via high-definition microphones. By our estimates and preliminary knowledge, the application is characterized by:

- High event rate ($\sim 1 Kevent/hour$), because of heavy traffic in dense urban areas.
- Big raw data footprint ($\sim 2 MiB/sample$), because noise sensors must sample some seconds of high-resolution stereophonic audio signal.
- High ML error rate ($\sim 35\%$), because of the involved bleeding-edge technology based on neural networks
- Long ML training times (~ 24 h @ $1 vCPU$), because of the involved complex models.

The cost breakdown for a deployment of $1K$ edge devices over 1 year is shown in Fig. 3. The main variable cost drivers are especially storage operations and then messaging. Computing and data transfer have a very small impact ($<1\%$) which is somewhat unexpected and needs further investigations: a possible reason could be our overly optimistic computing model.

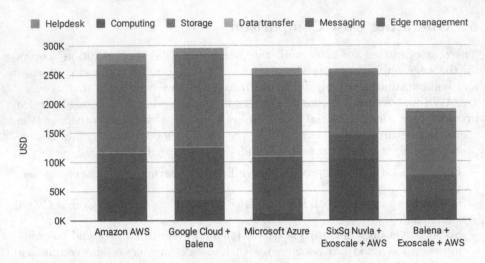

Fig. 3. Road Traffic Management: Cost breakdown for 1K-deployment over 1 year.

Scenario: Smart Grid. In this scenario, the edge devices forecast energy production and consumption by sampling electric power at several sensing stations in the same context-household, office, school, plant, etc. By our estimates and preliminary knowledge, the application is characterized by:

- Low event rate (~60 $event/hour$), because power measurements are normally averaged over a rather long time frames (minutes).
- Small raw data footprint (~0.1$MiB/sample$), because only power measurements are involved.
- Low ML error rate (~5%), because of proven and stable forecasting methods.
- Short ML training times (~ 4 h @ $1vCPU$), because forecasting is mainly based on simple models, such as XGBoost and LSTM.
- High ML training rate (~8 $round/month$), because the application needs to react quickly to context variations-changing weather, reduced consumption during unplanned absences, etc.

The cost breakdown for a deployment of 1K edge devices over 1 year is shown in Fig. 4. The main variable cost drivers are messaging and storage operations for two of the well-known providers; conversely, the edge management cost is dominating with AWS and the two newcomers. Again, computing and data transfer have a very small impact (<1%). Storage costs are negligible with the newcomer solutions because the adopted storage provider (Exoscale) does not charge for operations.

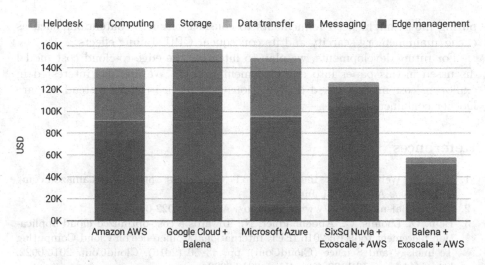

Fig. 4. Smart Grid: Cost breakdown for 1K-deployment over 1 year.

6   Conclusion

Large-scale IoT applications based on ML and employing self-adaptive algorithms call for cost-effective edge-to-cloud solutions. Indeed, this kind of systems poses challenges both at the Edge, because ML inference has to be performed efficiently on resource-constrained devices, and in the Cloud, because vast amounts of data have to be transferred and stored. Also, managing thousands of IoT and edge devices needs streamlined solutions for system monitoring and recurrent software updates.

Stakeholders wish to make informed decisions about the best PaaS Cloud platform for such deployments; thus, an analysis of the application requirements has been done to isolate the needed service components. Based on that, we proposed, as a first contribution, a generic reference service-oriented architecture as well as an event-driven application workflow, which we then mapped on selected Cloud platforms. Our second contribution is a detailed resource consumption model, based on PaaS pricing, which considers edge management, messaging, data transfer, storage space and operations, computing and helpdesk. We drew some cost estimates in two scenarios (Road Traffic Management, Smart Grid). The results show that the expenditure breakdown may vary significantly across the considered platform; among the variable costs, computing and data transfer have a very low impact compared to messaging and storage operations (space fees are negligible); the fixed costs (edge management and helpdesk) may dominate in scenarios characterized by a compact data footprint. The surprisingly low computing cost, especially in computationally-heavy scenarios like Road Traffic Management, might induce thinking that, contrarily to our expectations, dynamic AI (context-awareness and self-adaptation) has no significant incidence on overall expenditures. This demands more research: in fact, our simple computing model might need refinements to consider resource contentions such as cache/main memory scarcity and its consequent CPU stalling effects.

For future developments, we plan to integrate the edge-to-cloud cost model discussed in this paper into our placement tool [3]. We are also interested in exploring cost models based on Functions-as-a-Service (FaaS) instead of pure Docker containers.

References

1. Amazon Web Services Inc: AWS IoT Greengrass. https://aws.amazon.com/greengrass/. Accessed 01 June 2022
2. Balena: Balena. https://www.balena.io/. Accessed 2022-06-01
3. Belli, O., Loomis, C., Abdennadher, N.: Towards a cost-optimized cloud application placement tool. In: 2016 IEEE International Conference on Cloud Computing Technology and Science (CloudCom), pp. 43–50 (2016). CloudCom. 2016.0022. https://doi.org/10.1109/CloudCom.2016.0022
4. Google: Goolge Clouf IoT Core. https://cloud.google.com/iot-core. Accessed 01 June 2022
5. Goudarzi, M., Wu, H., Palaniswami, M., Buyya, R.: An application placement technique for concurrent iot applications in edge and fog computing environments. IEEE Trans. Mob. Comput. **20**(4), 1298–1311 (2021). https://doi.org/10.1109/TMC.2020.2967041
6. Laatikainen, G., Ojala, A., Mazhelis, O.: Cloud services pricing models. In: Herzwurm, G., Margaria, T. (eds.) ICSOB 2013. LNBIP, vol. 150, pp. 117–129. Springer, Heidelberg (2013). https://doi.org/10.1007/978-3-642-39336-5_12
7. Martens, B., Walterbusch, M., Teuteberg, F.: Costing of cloud computing services: a total cost of ownership approach. In: 2012 45th Hawaii International Conference on System Sciences, pp. 1563–1572 (2012). https://doi.org/10.1109/HICSS.2012.186. 186
8. Microsoft: Azure IoT Edge. https://azure.microsoft.com/en-us/services/iot-edge/. Accessed 01 June 2022
9. Nguyen, D.T., Pham, C., Nguyen, K.K., Cheriet, M.: Placement and chaining for run-time IoT service deployment in edge-cloud. IEEE Trans. Network Serv. Manage. **17**(1), 459–472 (2020). https://doi.org/10.1109/TNSM.2019.2948137. 2948137
10. Poleggi, M.E., Abdennadher, N., Dupuis, R., Mendonça, F.: Edge-to-cloud solutions for self-adaptive machine learning-based applications. Technical report. HEPIA - Haute école du paysage, d'ingénierie et d'architecture (2022)
11. SiqSq SA: Nuvla. https://sixsq.com/products-and-services/nuvla/overview. Accessed 01 June 2022

Exploring Blockchain-Based Management for LoRa IoT Nodes

Eloi Cruz Harillo and Felix Freitag[✉][iD]

Universitat Politècnica de Catalunya, BarcelonaTech, Barcelona, Spain
eloi.cruz@estudiantat.upc.edu, felix.freitag@upc.edu

Abstract. We consider open IoT applications in which the IoT devices, i.e. sensor nodes and gateways, can be contributed by volunteer participants. Since the contribution of sensor deployments and their data is critical for the value of such IoT applications, we propose to account for each participant her donation of both the measured data and the hardware, and translate this information into rewards to create incentives. The system architecture we propose uses a blockchain-based backend and aims to extend properties of the blockchain to the IoT sensor layer in order to achieve the trusted accounting of each contribution. A potential use case that can benefit from this concept are environmental monitoring applications that need to integrate IoT sensor nodes from third parties for increasing their geographic reach.

Keywords: LoRa · Blockchain · IoT

1 Introduction

Today's IoT applications often consist of full-stack applications that integrate sensor nodes which deliver the measured data. While most of the software is hosted at cloud-based services, the sensors are at remote locations, often without Internet access. Specific communication technologies of the IoT are used in order to connect these sensors with gateways. A popular solution for this communication is LoRa, a low power technology which can establish links of several kilometers between nodes and transmits small amounts of measurement data in LoRa packets [1].

Environmental monitoring applications are of a growing need for our society in order to better understand and control the effects of our actions on the surroundings. However, covering all monitoring needs by commercial IoT applications is costly and unfeasible for many stakeholders, such as communities of citizens, regional governments and municipalities. An alternative to a commercial solution is to build systems in which citizens can be involved, such as successfully shown in volunteer computing, where citizens contribute to scientific tasks [2]. For environmental monitoring applications this idea translates into open

J. Á. Bañares et al. (Eds.): GECON 2022, LNCS 13430, pp. 103–112, 2023.
https://doi.org/10.1007/978-3-031-29315-3_9

applications in which anybody can contribute with data and devices. Indeed, many valuable geographic locations of interest for data collection might be privately owned and are not publicly accessible, and the application would benefit if citizens are enabled to collaborate in the monitoring of the data. This later aspect relates to data collection from volunteer monitoring within citizen science [3].

The trustworthiness of the measured data in such open monitoring applications is critical for the data to be of value. Imagine a person that has the suspicion that a certain area is exposed to an elevated level of a pollutant. An open IoT application might be created driven by a citizen initiative in order to monitor this area. However, in order for the measured data to be of value, the data generated by the sensors needs to be trusted. While sensors can be calibrated to obtain correct measurements such as shown in [4], guarantees for the origin of the data and protection against manipulation, i.e. the immutability of the data, must be given by the design of the components of the system.

The challenge we address in this paper is the design of components for an open IoT application to achieve a trusted accounting of the contributions of sensors and gateways by participants to an IoT network, in order to use this information for being able to incentivize such contributions with rewards. We present the prototype of a system based on the vision of LoRaCoin [5], which consists of a blockchain-based application to manage IoT sensors of a low-power wide-area network. The system aims to account both for IoT sensor nodes that generate the data and the gateways that provide the Internet connectivity to these sensor nodes.

2   Background and Related Work

One of the successful applications of blockchain is its use for the decentralized accounting of contributions. Several practical applications such as GridCoin[1], to reward volunteer computing contributions, and FileCoin[2], to reward storage contributions, are used in production with real communities of users. The concept is that third parties can contribute their computing resources to a system, the system measures this contribution, and the amount of the contribution is rewarded with coins. Blockchain technology is used to transparently account the contribution and to create specific coins that are rewarded.

Blockchain-based smart contracts can also be used to perform tasks of coordination of resources. In [6] blockchain is proposed to support the management of a pool of edge computing resources in an IoT application. In that work the KubeEdge container orchestration engine integrates an interface with smart contracts in order to provision edge resources for running software components on demand. The benefit are IoT applications which can more flexibly adapt to execution time and power consumption requirements. An operational application

---

[1] https://gridcoin.us/.
[2] https://filecoin.io/.

example in which the coordination capacity derived from the blockchain is leveraged is the provision of computing resources offered through a marketplace in iExec[3].

Incentivizing the provision of IoT hardware, specifically LoRa gateways, is the objective of the Helium network[4]. Different from the above mentioned examples of GridCoin, Filecoin and iExec, in which computing resources connected to the Internet are contributed at the exchange of coins, in Helium the target is that third parties contribute LoRa gateways, which enable that data from sensor nodes can reach the Internet. It is interesting to mention in this context that LoRa is a technology that does not need any licence or network operator, different for instance to NB-IoT or Sigfox. Due to this fact IoT applications that integrate LoRa networks have the potential to grow organically in the IoT layer with the contributions from everybody.

Most IoT applications which integrate a LoRa-based network apply the LoRaWAN standard [7]. In LoRaWAN, the LoRa network consists of LoRa gateways and LoRa end nodes. LoRa gateways have two network interfaces, one northbound connected to the Internet and one southbound to receive LoRa packets. The end nodes (e.g. sensor nodes) do not have Internet connectivity and use LoRa communication to reach the gateway. The gateway transmits the received data messages to higher levels of the IoT application.

Possibly the largest worldwide deployment of LoRaWAN-based IoT applications has been done through The Things Network (TTN)[5], which reports to have nowadays more than 170k members and more than 20k gateways. While the company offers an Enterprise Edition, the Things Stack Community Edition is popular among makers for registering LoRaWAN nodes and gateways of personal IoT applications which then leverage the centralized backend services of The Things Industries.

Several works have combined blockchain with LoRa-based IoT applications. In [8] a decentralized pollution monitoring system based on blockchain is proposed. The authors detail a list of non-functional requirements that need to be fulfilled in order to achieve trusted data from the IoT nodes. Another IoT pollution monitoring system using LoRaWAN and blockchain is presented in [9]. The focus is on applying smart contracts of the Ethereum blockchain to provide data integrity without the need for a Trusted Third Party. In the work of Ribero et al. [10] a permissioned blockchain is used to replace a component of the LoRaWAN stack, specifically the Join Server, responsible for the management of the keys of the LoRa nodes. The benefit of the solution is avoiding a single point of failure while similar execution and latencies are obtained. In our preliminary work described in [5] we introduced the idea of LoRaCoin. Our current work builds upon that early vision and describes the developed prototype.

---

[3] https://iex.ec/.
[4] https://www.helium.com/.
[5] https://www.thethingsnetwork.org/.

3   Application Design

3.1   Architectural Overview

A LoRa-based IoT application typically consists of the IoT device layer where data is produced, a gateway layer which interconnects the data from the IoT devices with the Internet, and a cloud-based backend where the data is processed, analyzed and stored.

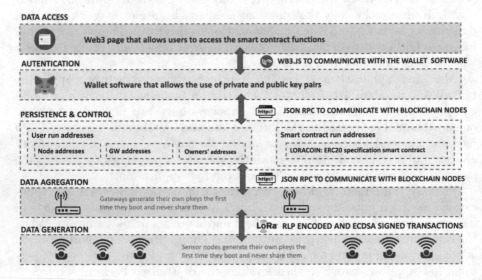

Fig. 1. Overview layered architecture.

Figure 1 gives an overview of the architectural layers on which our application design is based. The two layers at the bottom, i.e. the data generation and data aggregation layer, correspond to the functions performed by the IoT devices of the application. The nodes in the data generation layer obtain sensor data that is transmitted by LoRa packets to the gateway. The gateways, belonging to the data aggregation layer, have Internet connectivity and are able to communicate these data to higher layers of the application. The persistence and control layer is formed by the smart contracts hosted on the blockchain, providing both persistence of data and control of the operations. The authentication layer is required to validate certain write operations performed by the the smart contracts. For the authentication the Elliptic Curve Digital Signature Algorithm (ECDSA) is used. This has an interesting effect as it removes the need for the users to be registered to the platform and thus disclosing personal information. The data access refers to the graphical frontend of the application to perform the user-oriented interactions.

3.2   Functional Analysis

We analyze several functions of the application with regards to the interaction of the components in the prototype.

Creating an IoT Device: All IoT devices that connect to the smart contract of the application have to be created before. Creating a device is done by adding the device address to a list of valid devices kept by the smart contract. The function *createDevice* of the communication interface of the smart contract is invoked for this purpose. This call can only be made by the provider of the device. The steps are as follows: The device runs a routine which creates its address that then appears at the OLED screen. Through the application's graphical user interface, the hardware provider registers the address of the device which is stored in a variable of the smart contract. Initially, the authorized hardware providers are registered at the smart contact.

Rewarding a Sensor Node Owner for Data Contributions: The transactions containing sensor data are produced when LoRa nodes capture data that is send to the gateway and from there to the smart contract. As step 1 it is necessary that a gateway is made available that provides network coverage to the LoRa sensor node. This gateway then is able to receive LoRa packets from its LoRa interface. In case of being it a first interaction between sensor node and gateway, the next two steps are performed: When the node initializes for the first time (step 2), it generates a private key that is saved in the flash memory. The key is used to sign transactions. In step 3 the sensor node sends a signed message to the gateway and from there this message is sent to the smart contract for the gateway to obtain confirmation that the sensor node is a registered device. In step 4 the sensor node sends a signed message to the gateway to validate that the gateway is a registered device. The gateway sends a signed acknowledgement back to the node which in addition contains the signature of the hardware provider, allowing the LoRa node to validate the gateway. After having done this mutual validation, the LoRa node sends a LoRa data packet to the gateway in step 5, which is encapsulated in the http requests that the gateway sends to the smart contract. After registering the data, in step 6 the node owner is rewarded.

Rewarding a Gateway Owner for the Relaying of a Data Message: When the gateway sends a message to the smart contract, it is validated by the signatures contained in the message and a transaction is written to the blockchain by *sendTransaction* whose hash is returned to the gateway. In order for the gateway to claim the reward, the gateway invokes the method *registerTransaction* with the parameter that contains the previously obtained hash. That allows to validate the contribution of the gateway and then to release the reward.

4   Prototype

We implement a prototype and deploy the frontend and backend in a local environment. As described in Sect. 3.1, the backend of the application is formed by the layer of control and persistence. This layer is implemented by a decentralised service which hosts the smart contracts. Typically, testnets are used for testing application that use the Ethereum blockchain. In our case, we use the Ganache blockchain environment, which provides to the application the same interfaces as the production Ethereum blockchain.

We use real IoT devices for prototyping the IoT layer, specifically the TTGO T-Beam embedded system board which feature an ESP32 microcontroller and a SX1276 LoRa transceiver. The device is flashed with code to be either a gateway or a sensor node. The sensor nodes are deployed in a star topology around a gateway as shown in Fig. 2. The LoRa technology is used for the communication between the sensor nodes and the gateway.

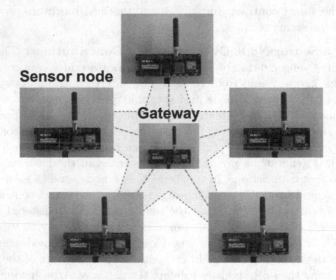

Fig. 2. Deployment of IoT nodes in a star topology.

The smart contracts deployed on the blockchain provide the control and data persistence for the application. Figure 3 contains a code fragment of the smart contract that is implemented in our prototype. First a set of variables can be seen, which contain the state of the application which evolves by the invocation of the methods of the smart contract. Then a set of methods are declared for the management of the devices, corresponding to the different use cases of the application, some of which have been described in Sect. 3.2. Finally, the smart contract contains a set of methods for managing data messages. These methods allow to relate the received data messages to the contributions of the sensor nodes and enable the accounting.

The frontend of the application is given by Web pages and corresponds to the data access layer of the architecture described in Sect. 3.1. Node.js is used

```
1  contract LoraCoin is ERC20 {
2
3      address public root;
4
5      struct NetworkDevice {
6          address owner;
7          bytes signature;
8          bytes32[] transactions;
9      }
10     mapping(address=>NetworkDevice) public devices;
11
12     constructor(string, string) ERC20(name, symbol);
13
14     //Device management
15     function createDevice(address _address, bytes ←
            memory _signature) public returns (bool);
16     function registerDevice(address _address, uint8 ←
            v, bytes32 r, bytes32 s) public returns (bool←
            );
17     function getDevices() public view returns (←
            address [ ] memory)
18     function getOwnerDevices() public view returns (←
            address [ ] memory);
19
20     //Data management
21     function sendTransaction(bytes memory data) ←
            public returns(bool);
22     function registerTransaction(address ←
            _sensorAddress, bytes32 transactionHash) ←
            public returns(bool);
23 }
```

Fig. 3. Code fragment of the implemented smart contract.

to provide the Web page which is shown in Fig. 4 (left). It can be seen in this example that three devices have been registered. The devices have both their proper Ethereum address, which is registered by the hardware provider after the device is created (as explained in Sect. 3.2), as well as the owner address in case the device has been purchased, as shown for the first device.

The operations of the smart contract which produce a transaction, e.g. by writing to a variable and changing its state, result in a cost. This cost is paid by the account corresponding to the Ethereum address which desires to generate the transaction. To perform the transaction it is needed that the request is signed. We use the Metamask wallet, which manages the private keys belonging to the users' Ethereum accounts. Figure 4 (right) shows the Metamask interface for such an Ethereum account. It can be seen that this account has already made operations in the prototype application, since 10 LRC (LoRaCoins) have been gained as a reward.

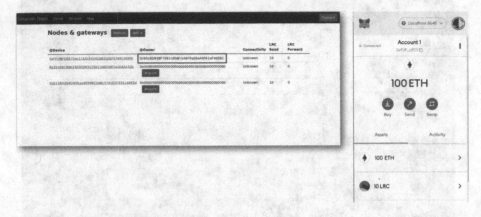

Fig. 4. Left: Web application frontend. Right: Metamask wallet of a rewarded device owner.

The result of the prototype experimentation is the demonstration of a proof-of-concept implementation of the application. The design, which assigns Ethereum addresses to the involved actors, i.e. nodes, gateways and owners, along with private and public key pairs associated to each of these accounts for the signing and authentication of messages, allows to attribute the operations performed on the smart contracts with their respective accounts, and thus the accounting of each actor's contribution.

The design decisions taken, however, have also implied a trade-off on how open the application actually is to the different types of participation. Principally, the application is open for participants which desire to contribute as data and gateway providers. They can participate if they have an Ethereum account, and through the application they can become the owner of a device (Fig. 4 left) and contribute data. Our design, however, has achieved less flexibility with regards to the registration of any IoT hardware. Each IoT node that operates in the application has to be created beforehand by a registered hardware provider. On one hand, this registration enables that the node obtains an Etherum address and a public and private key pair, allowing the application to validate for any operation that it is performed by a valid node. On the other hand, this solution does not allow that a user can register any new hardware, but only those IoT devices that are known to the application can be used.

5   Conclusions

This paper addressed the concept of creating a blockchain-based accounting system for incentivizing third party contributions to open IoT applications. The scenario considered are IoT applications open to participation, to which anybody can contribute by providing IoT hardware or IoT data. Environmental monitoring applications were given as a case for which the participatory contribution of a large number of IoT nodes for delivering measurements can be specifically useful.

A prototype of the system was implemented and demonstrated by the deployment of a proof-of-concept. A blockchain-based backend was used for the control and data persistence layer of the application. A key design decision was to create Ethereum addresses together with their associated public and private key pairs for all the involved actors. This allowed that the operations done with the application through the smart contracts could be correctly attributed to the specific actor involved, and as a consequence, the contribution could be accounted for being rewarded.

While the developed system focused on being able to account contribution in terms of hardware and measured data for incentivizing participation, it could be interesting to further research how to give value to these measured data and how valuable each sensor node is. The current system design assures that a received message with measured data is indeed sent from a registered sensor node. If in addition the value of these data was known, then the reward given could be tailored to the data sent, encouraging thus not only data contributions, but also fostering the contributions of those nodes which are more useful.

Acknowledgements. This project has received funding from the European Union's Horizon 2020 research and innovation programme under grant agreement No 957228— TruBlo and was partially supported by the Spanish Government under contracts PID2019-106774RB-C21, PCI2019-111851-2 (LeadingEdge CHIST-ERA), PCI2019-111850-2 (DiPET CHIST-ERA).

References

1. Haxhibeqiri, J., De Poorter, E., Moerman, I., Hoebeke, J.: A survey of LoRaWAN for IoT: from technology to application. Sensors **18**(11), 3995 (2018)
2. Anderson, D.: BOINC: a platform for volunteer computing. J Grid Comput. **18**, 99–122 (2020)
3. Wiggins, A., Wilbanks, J.: The rise of citizen science in health and biomedical research. Am. J. Bioeth. **19**(8), 3–14 (2019). PMID: 31339831
4. Ferrer-Cid, P., Barcelo-Ordinas, J.M., Garcia-Vidal, J., Ripoll, A., Viana, M.: Multisensor data fusion calibration in IoT air pollution platforms. IEEE Internet Things J. **7**(4), 3124–3132 (2020)
5. Cruz Harillo, E., Freitag, F.: Poster abstract: LoRACoin: towards a blockchain-based platform for managing LoRa devices. In: IEEE INFOCOM 2022 - IEEE Conference on Computer Communications Workshops (INFOCOM WKSHPS), pp. 1–2 (2022)
6. Zhou, M.T., Shen, F.G., Ren, T.F., Feng, X.Y.: Blockchain-based volunteer edge cloud for IoT applications. In: 2021 IEEE 93rd Vehicular Technology Conference (VTC2021-Spring), pp. 1–6 (2021)

7. Almuhaya, M.A.M., Jabbar, W.A., Sulaiman, N., Abdulmalek, S.: A survey on LoRaWAN technology: recent trends, opportunities, simulation tools and future directions. Electronics **11**(1), 164 (2022)
8. Lücking, M., et al.: The merits of a decentralized pollution-monitoring system based on distributed ledger technology. IEEE Access **8**, 189365–189381 (2020)
9. Niya, S.R., Jha, S.S., Bocek, T., Stiller, B.: Design and implementation of an automated and decentralized pollution monitoring system with blockchains, smart contracts, and LoRaWAN. In: NOMS 2018–2018 IEEE/IFIP Network Operations and Management Symposium, pp. 1–4 (2018)
10. Ribeiro, V., Holanda, R., Ramos, A., Rodrigues, J.J.P.C.: Enhancing key management in LoRaWAN with permissioned blockchain. Sensors **20**(11), 3068 (2020)

A Serverless Computing Platform
for Software Defined Networks

Fatemeh Banaie and Karim Djemame (✉)

School of Computing, University of Leeds, Leeds LS2 9JT, UK
K.Djemame@leeds.ac.uk

Abstract. Recent advances in network management strategies, namely the possibility of network programmability through the use of Software-Defined Networking (SDN) increase the velocity of network evolutions. SDN promises a software-based networking approach, where software modules are used to abstract network functionalities. To achieve this aim, the virtualization paradigm can be used in these modules within the context of Network Function Virtualisation (NFV). NFV plays the most important role in transition toward open software and network hardware. Given the promise of these technologies, micro-services can greatly benefit from the integration of SDN and NFV and execute in a suitable cloud platform. This paper describes a modular, and micro-service based SDN architecture that applies network programmability within the context of NFV and explores how it could benefit from the serverless computing paradigm. Serverless computing accompanies modular SDN in building cost-effective, energy-aware, and scalable networks, relieving the management burden of network maintenance.

Keywords: network management · open-source software · Software Defined Networks · serverless computing · Network Function Virtualization

1 Introduction

Software-Defined Networking (SDN) and Network Functions Virtualization (NFV) are new paradigms in the move towards open software and network hardware [1]. SDN aims to accelerate the design and implementation of the next generation computer networks. It decouples vertical integration of the control plane and data plane and provides flexibility that allows software to program the data plane hardware directly according to a set of network policies. SDNs have the ability to facilitate the containerised applications and network traffic consolidation to optimise not only performance but energy consumption as well [2].

Serverless Computing [3] offers the illusion of infinite resources that are dynamically provisioned by cloud providers, allowing users to invest less effort and capital in infrastructure management. Moreover, a serverless computing system is an ideal solution to build and optimise any Internet of Things (IoT) operations with zero infrastructure and maintenance costs and little-to-no operating expense [4].

J. Á. Bañares et al. (Eds.): GECON 2022, LNCS 13430, pp. 113–123, 2023.
https://doi.org/10.1007/978-3-031-29315-3_10

The SDN controllers are a great fit for the serverless computing paradigm as they are highly event-driven, modular, and parallel [5]. Moreover, serverless computing provides a resource-efficient, low overhead alternative to Virtual Machines (VMs) and containers, and can effectively support SDN and function virtualisation. Network function virtualisation (NFV) decouples networking software from the hardware that delivers it so that software can evolve independently [5].

The integrated SDN/NFV architecture deployed on a serverless platform can accelerate the innovation and deployment of network services. A serverless function is essentially a proxy for energy usage as a unit of (serverless) compute and therefore a cost, making network functions instantiation and orchestration significantly energy and resource efficient [2]. Therefore, this research aims at realizing the concept of modular SDN based on serverless functions with the goal to implement a novel platform to reduce the energy consumption of applications deployment and operation on the Internet [2]. The platform's new building blocks are made of 1) a methodology combining SDN, NFV and serverless architectures; 2) placement algorithms for serverless functions to minimise energy consumption; 3) the underlying software implementation.

This paper explores the technical issues and implementation of the proposed SDN/NFV architecture as a first step. The following summarizes its main contributions:

- We propose a micro-service based SDN/NFV architecture, where network services can be deployed as serverless functions. The proposed architecture leverages the virtualisation technology in deploying network functions on a serverless platform. Consequently, this architecture disaggregates the network functionalities so that the SDN controller only provides the minimum required functionalities, and the other network services can be deployed on zero infrastructure with a little-to-no operating expense.
- The proposed architecture is implemented using the well-known open network operating system (ONOS) [6] and function as service (OpenFaaS) serverless platform [7].

The rest of the paper is organized as follows. Section 2 provides a brief overview of the related literature. In Sect. 3, we briefly describe the proposed architecture used in this paper. Section 4 describes the details of implementation. Section 5 demonstrates and discusses the evaluation results, followed by a conclusion in Sect. 6.

2   Related Work

Related work snaps in the area of how to overcome the challenges that rise from deploying SDN and whether the underlying network services could be efficiently delivered, managed, and disseminated to the end users. This includes SDN integration with serverless architecture. Reference [8] provides insights into key factors such as the computational resources, the number of Virtual Network Functions (VNFs) running on a VM, and their resource demands affecting the performance of VNFs that are hosted in virtualized system architectures. Reference [9] also provides an overview of NFV-based service development and requirements that are addressed in existing Service Development Kits (SDKs).

Some open-source implementations of SDN adopt a monolithic software approach besides utilizing the concept of VNFs in service delivery such as ONOS and OpenDaylight (ODL) [10]. For example, ODL can provide agile service delivery on OpenStack cloud infrastructures by implementing services using NFV. However, recent studies have started to move towards a microservices-based architecture. Reference [11] presents a distributed architecture for the design and implementation of SDN control plane systems that split the current monolithic controller software into a set of cooperating microservices, which can be implemented in different (and appropriate) programming languages. The architecture supports the distribution of events to external processes. In this regard, some studies focus on SDN-based strategies to manage the network efficiently, especially in the case of smart IoT applications, e.g., to leverage a SDN-based approach to satisfy the latency requirements of the services in multi-access edge computing applications [12]. However, these approaches do not aim to design a modular SDN architecture, but rather focus on utilizing SDN for managing distributed applications in an edge environment.

The adaptation of the serverless and Function as a Service (FaaS) paradigm in an edge environment was introduced in [13], where key issues and high-level directions were proposed, and different types of deployment and a serverless platform were discussed. This was supported by a prototype implemented with the open-source serverless solution OpenWhisk [14] and open source products.

In [15], a framework is proposed for efficient dispatching of stateless tasks with the goal of minimizing the response times and exhibiting short and long-term fairness. Their evaluation of the OpenWisk platform shows that the interaction with SDN controller can be useful in relieving network congestion. A high-performance serverless platform for NFV is presented in [16], in which the authors utilize three different mechanisms for minimizing the latency, including state management, efficient NF execution model, and avoiding packet latency. The work presented in [18] focuses on energy efficiency by decomposing the application into fine-grained functions.

3   A FaaS Architecture for Modular SDN

Network management strategies are undergoing a transition from using the proprietary technology of a vendor toward the open-source software modules with service automation. The first glimmer of this transformation is SDN that increases the velocity of network evolutions by delivering new network capabilities. SDN aims to decouple the control plane and data plane for scalability and easier network management. The control plane consists of SDN core functionalities (e.g. topology service, flow service, inventory service, etc.) and management applications (e.g. firewall, load balancing, routing, monitoring, etc.), which communicate requirements via Northbound Application Program Interfaces (API).

The data plane consists of forwarding elements (i.e., switches and routers) and uses OpenFlow [19] as Southbound API.

SDN controller operates by serving the events from both the southbound and northbound APIs. These events can be defined as any changes in the network that lead to invoking one or more SDN's management applications. Therefore, the SDN controller can be designed as an event-driven and modular software that operates by responding to these events. The management applications can be deployed on a serverless platform and can be executed whenever required. However, the monolithic design of current SDN controllers aggregates all functions into a single and huge program. This approach restricts its ability to deploy a new service, independent of other services. As a result, a modular and micro-service based SDN architecture [11] deployed on a serverless platform is developed as illustrated in Fig. 1, which applies network programmability within the context of NFV. In this approach, SDN core services provide minimum required functionality, and the other services can be provided by external applications in the form of a set of cooperating software modules. These modules can be implemented as a set of independent functions (network functions) that leverage the benefits of the serverless computing paradigm in providing on-demand scalability and efficient resource management.

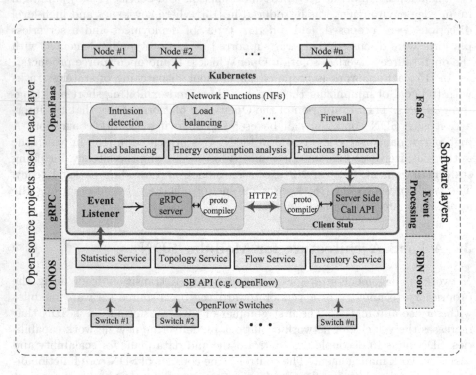

Fig. 1. A FaaS architecture for modular SDN.

The FaaS paradigm provides a platform to develop applications as a set of independent functions. It accelerates application deployment by eliminating the need for managing infrastructure, thus can be well suited for our SDN/NFV architecture. Moreover, FaaS eliminates the management burden of resource allocation (i.e., choosing the right time as well as the right type of VMs, and containers) and further reduces costs. Accordingly, users only provide network functions (which are SDN microservices) to this platform. Upon receiving an event from Application APIs, the platform start executing the services automatically by deploying new instances. Network developers no longer need to consider function deployment, management, and scaling issues. Besides reducing the management burden, network service providers are charged according to the number of events in the NFV context and therefore only pay for what they use at a very fine granularity [16]. The next section gives details of the implementation of the architecture. The associated source code is available in the GitHub repository[1].

4   Implementation

This section presents the software components and technologies leveraged in implementing the serverless SDN/NFV architecture. We utilized three well-known open-source projects, i.e., Open Network Operating System (ONOS) [6], general-purpose Remote Procedure Call (gRPC) [20], and Functions as a Service (OpenFaaS) [7], for implementing our model's layer, respectively. As can be seen in Fig. 1, the architecture consists of three main components including:

- Event listening module in SDN layer which is responsible for catching an OpenFlow-based events coming from mininet and forwarding them toward OpenFaaS connector.
- Event processing module that uses a communication interface to notify ONOS events to the VNF deployed on OpenFaaS. This module provides the ability of interacting with the virtual functions via gRPC protocol.
- Microservice handling module in the serverless layer that manages the functions and invocations by receiving event notifications from underlying network.

ONOS is an open-source SDN controller developed by open networking foundation (ONF). It has a layered structure in its architectural design including the application, core and providers/protocols layers. Applications use a collection of Northbound Interfaces (NBI) to stay informed about the events and network states. ONOS services are implemented in the core part, where it manages the network states and notifies the applications by occurring the relevant changes in states. These services also provide an inventory of currently connected devices, hosts, links, and an overview of the current network topology, along with the rules installed in the devices. The lowest layer of ONOS stack consists of the Southbound Interface (SBI), where a collection of plugins resides including a

---

[1] https://github.com/EDGNSS.

provider interface with protocol-specific libraries and a service interface. It is responsible for interacting with the network environment using various control and configuration protocols. The mininet environment is used for emulating the underlying network such as switches and hosts as well as generating network packets coming from data plane [17].

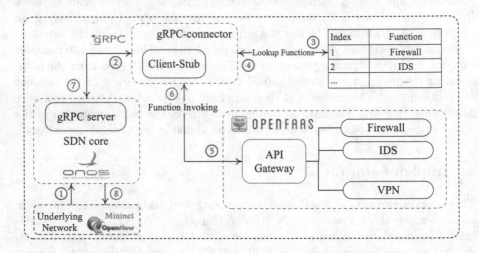

Fig. 2. ONOS and OpenFaaS Integration Sequense Diagram.

In ONOS, the events are used to notify the listening applications about the changes in network. According to the service structure in ONOS, we leverage the benefits of an event distribution system to externalize event processing in SDN [11]. This allows us to divide the control plane services into a set of cooperating microservices, where the minimum required services are provided by core and the extra functionalities can be served by microservices which are implemented on OpenFaaS (Fig. 2).

These microservices can be deployed as web services using VNFs in a distributed environment. The event listener and virtual functions are communicating (e.g. sending and receiving event notifications) through the communication interface. The communication interface used in this project is based on opensource communication interfaces. So, the next component of our event processing layer is the gRPC protocol that is used for connecting these microservices. gRPC is an open-source RPC system based on a protocol buffer that uses HTTP/2 as its underlying transport protocol. It has a lot of interesting features such as security, authentication mechanism, bidirectional streaming, etc. It also allows us to automatically generate the required code for both the server and client sides. Moreover, gRPC provides faster information exchange due to the compressed data packing of the Protocol Buffers and the use of HTTP/2. We have implemented a gRPC server as the ONOS application, where it makes a call to ONOS services and turned the returned value into protobuf form, serializes, and sends it to the client.

The client stub is implemented as an external application, named gRPC-connector to OpenFaas, that connects ONOS services to OpenFaaS Functions. OpenFaaS is a popular open-source serverless platform that makes it easy for developers to deploy event-driven functions with docker and Kubernetes. Open-Faas functions and microservices can be easily invoked by any kind of event, for example, HTTP is one of the use cases that can connect systems. They are accessible over HTTP endpoints via the Gateway service. Upon receiving an event from ONOS, the connector queries the list of functions in Gateway and then builds a map between the event's topic and the existing functions, which leads to triggering the respective function on a given topic.

5   Evaluation

5.1   Results and Discussion

To evaluate the performance of SDN/NFV architecture, we deploy the architecture on two servers with 4 VCPUs, 16 GB memory running on Microsoft Azure. The first server runs onos with grpc-server installed on it, along with mininet which emulates a network with 8 openflow-enabled switches and hosts. The second server runs OpenFaaS which is used as a resource pool and network functions host. These two servers are connected via 1Gbps LAN network and run Ubuntu 20.04 LTS. At first, the feasibility of the modular and distributed architecture is investigated by deploying a simple serverless forwarding application (used for packet processing for every new packet arriving at the controller). In this scenario, once a host sends a ping request for which there is not any established forwarding rule, the switch directs the incoming packet to the SDN controller. The event listening module of the controller serves the packet by sending it to the external application deployed on a serverless platform via a gRPC channel. The deployed function can process the packet to find the source and destination addresses of the packet.

Furthermore, the performance of the proposed architecture is reported through some preliminary results considering various scenarios. The objective of the evaluation is to compare the performance of the proposed distributed architecture implementation with a monolithic one that hosts local applications. A host sends a continuous flow of IP packets, which generates the event notification in the controller, and accordingly leads a function to be invoked on OpenFaaS. In this experiment, ONOS communication with VNFs is handled via gRPC protocol and the OpenFaaS orchestrates the function requests by an automatic scaling process. We have conducted the experimental evaluation of our model through a diverse set of serverless workloads. To do so, the traffic load is increased during experiments to observe the behavior of both models in higher traffic arrivals. Figure 3(a) illustrates the effect of the number of packets per second on the mean response time recorded during the experiment. Each observation shows the latency in both the control plane and the VNFs layer.

As can be seen, the mean response times of the local functions are lower than serverless-based functions at the start of the experiment. The reason for this is

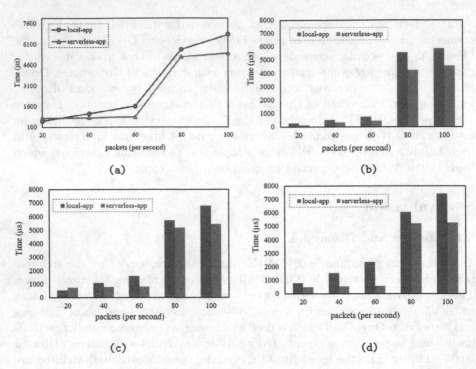

Fig. 3. The Average delay in: (a) different arrival rates. (b) service rate $= \frac{1}{b} = 25\,\mu s$. (c) service rate $\frac{1}{b} = 34\,\mu s$. (d) service rate $\frac{1}{b} = 42\,\mu s$.

the latency imposed by grpc channel to invoke the remote functions on Open-Faas. Furthermore, both applications (i.e., local and remote functions) experience a higher amount of response times with increasing the arrival rate of packets on the data plane, because it imposes a higher processing load in the network. However, it is observed that the serverless-based approach outperforms the local method in higher packet arrivals, as it can automatically scale and manage the resources according to the workload.

In the second scenario, we have considered the latency in different service rates of the functions, which is due to the processing of the different packet sizes. Figure 3(b) compares the results in mean processing time of $\frac{1}{b} = 25\,\mu s$ for both local and serverless-based applications. As observed, the mean delay of both applications shows an up trend. However, it is lower for serverless-based application than the local one with the results for local functions showing a steep slope. Furthermore, with increasing the processing time of the function in Fig. 3(c) to $\frac{1}{b} = 34\,\mu s$, local functions win at low packet arrivals, but experience higher amounts of delay with increasing the arrival rate. As discussed previously, the reason is due to the scalability of the serverless platform, which can also be seen from Fig. 3(d) in $\frac{1}{b} = 42\,\mu s$. Intuitively, the higher the workload in each experiment is, the more important the ability of scaling becomes. These results can clearly show the benefits of the serverless-based method in latency handling and service scaling.

5.2 Extensions

In this paper, a modular and distributed SDN framework that paves the way to manage a novel paradigm of microservices-based applications in designing the next generation IoT networks is presented. As such, the use of microservices represents a big step ahead in the vision of serverless edge architectures. However, the serverless paradigm still requires addressing special challenges to enhance its applicability across all phases of the general application landscape, including network security services. The following improvements can be considered to support the proposed architecture:

- As *energy consumption* is a vital issue in distributed systems, employing edge computing with low-powered computing resources contributes to more energy-efficient system development. Moreover, an energy aware automatic serverless functions instantiation and orchestration framework for edge computing environments is currently being implemented. In this context, a resource mapping algorithm is necessary to address the energy efficiency in the serverless platform by appropriately selecting the server nodes (i.e., the right CPU cores to run the functions) and the placement of functions. Functions taking up the most execution time can be identified, which equals *cost*.
- The modules in an SDN controller are implemented and deployed as separate, stand-alone serverless functions. Accordingly, a suitable task scheduling method can enable on-demand *scaling up/down* of the functions with regards to their workload in an energy-aware environment [21].
- To avoid start-up latency, the underlying virtualisation technology must be optimised to decrease the start-up latency of *cold* start launching in a selverless platform. This can be tackled by suitable managing of the function instances in this platform, e.g., reusing launched instances by keeping them *warm* for a period of time [21], or reduction of the container image size.
- Network functions are usually short-lived and in most scenarios, they are chained together to form a Service Function Chain (SFC). The development and performance tuning of SCFs are difficult and should be considered in designing the more complex application scenarios.
- An effective *load balancing* algorithm can also manage the resource utilisation by distributing the function executions to the available resources, which can further improve the performance of the system in terms of energy expenditure and service delivery latency. However, load balancing approaches may not necessarily enhance the performance of group functions in SFC due to the loss of locality [5]. In other word, the locality requirements must be considered to group functions as a single application to provide faster data sharing among interacting functions.

6 Conclusion

This paper presents a microservices-based distributed architecture for implementing SDN controller in order to improve agility, scalability, and performance in the network. The SDN features such as the possibility of network programmability and reconfiguration according to the application requirements make it a key enabler for the upcoming next-generation IoT networks. However, the limitations of the existing monolithic SDN architecture restrict it to fulfil the needs of IoT applications in terms of scalability and performance. In particular, a good system design needs modularity, so, a modular and microservice-based SDN architecture is required to tackle these limitations in distributed system environments such as IoT applications.

The experimental results show that the serverless paradigm can decrease service latency for disaggregated architectures, and also provide on-demand and scalable resource management. The reduction in the execution time and the average resource usage of microservices allows for many optimizations from the resource management point of view.

Acknowledgements. The authors would like to thank the European Next Generation Internet Program for Open INTErnet Renovation (NGI-Pointer 2) for supporting this work under contract 871528 (EDGENESS Project).

References

1. Bonfim, M.S., Dias, K.L., Fernandes, F.L.: Integrated NFV/SDN architectures: a systematic literature review. ACM Comput. Surv. **51**(6), 1–39 (2019)
2. Djemame, Karim: Energy efficiency in edge environments: a serverless computing approach. In: Tserpes, K. (ed.) GECON 2021. LNCS, vol. 13072, pp. 181–184. Springer, Cham (2021). https://doi.org/10.1007/978-3-030-92916-9_15
3. Kiritikos, K., Skrzypek, P.: A review of serverless frameworks. In: 2018 IEEE/ACM International Conference on Utility and Cloud Computing, pp. 161–168 (2018)
4. Gorbmann, M., Ioannidis, C., Le, D.: Applicability of serverless computing in fog computing environments for IoT scenarios. In: Proceedings of the 12th IEEE/ACM International Conference on Utility and Cloud Computing, Auckland, New Zealand, pp. 29–34. ACM (2019)
5. Aditya, P., et al.: Will serverless computing revolutionized NFV? Proc. IEEE **107**(4), 667–678 (2019)
6. Berde, P., et al.: ONOS: towards an open, distributed SDN OS. In: HotSDN 2014: Proceedings of the Third Workshop on Hot Topics in Software Defined Networking, pp. 1–6. ACM (2014)
7. OpenFaas. Serverless functions made simple (2019). https://github.com/openfaas/faas
8. Falkner, M., Leivadeas, A., Lambadaris, I., Kesidis, G.: Performance analysis of virtualise network functions on virtualized systems architectures. In: 2016 IEEE 21th International Workshop on Computer Aided Modelling and Design of Communication Links and Networks (CAMAD), pp. 71–76 (2016)
9. Ustok, R.F., et al.: Service development kit for media-type virtualized network services in 5G networks. IEEE Commun. Mag. **58**(7), 51–57 (2020)
10. OpenDaylight: OpenDaylight and Open Networking ecosystem. https://www.opendaylight.org
11. Cormer, D., Rastegarnia, A.: Toward dissagregating the SDN control plane. IEEE Commun. Mag. **57**(10), 70–75 (2019)

12. Fondo-Ferreiro, P., et al.: A software-defined networking solution for transparent session and service continuity in dynamic multi-access edge computing. IEEE Trans. Netw. Serv. Manage. **18**(2), 1401–1414 (2020)
13. Baresi, L., Mendonca, D.F., Garriga, M., Guinea, S., Quattrocchi, G.: A unified model for the mobile-edge-cloud continuum. ACM Trans. Internet Technol. **19**(2), 1–21 (2019)
14. Djemame, K., Parker, M., Datsev, D.: Open-source serverless architecture: an evaluation of apache openwhisk. In: 2020 IEEE/ACM 13th International Conference on Utility and Cloud Computing (UCC), pp. 329–335 (2020)
15. Cicconetti, C., Conti, M., Passarella, A.: A decentralized framework for serverless edge computing in the internet of things. IEEE Trans. Netw. Serv. Manage. **18**(2), 2166–2180 (2021)
16. Shen, J., Yu, H., Zheng, Z., Sun, C., Xu, M., Wang, J.: Serpens: a high-performance serverless platform for NFV. In: 2020 IEEE/ACM 28th International Symposium on Quality of Service (IWQoS), pp. 1–10 (2020)
17. Download/Get Started with Mininet (2017). http://mininet.org/download
18. Tzenetopoulos, A., Marantos, C., Gavrielides, G., Xydis, S., Soudris, D.: FADE: FAAS-inspired application decomposition and energy aware function placement on the edge, pp. 7–10. Association for Computing Machinery, New York (2021)
19. Singhvi, A., Khalid, J., Akella, A., Banerjee, S.: SNF: serverless network functions. In: ACM Symposium on Cloud Computing (2020)
20. grpc: A high performance, open source, general-purpose RPC framework (2016). https://github.com/grpc
21. Li, Z., Guo, L., Cheng, J., Chen, Q., He, B., Guo, M.: The serverless computing survey: a technical primer for design architecture. ACM Comput. Surv. **54**, 1–34 (2022)

Edge Computing Applications in Industrial IoT: A Literature Review

Alp Bayar[1]([⊠]) [iD], Umut Şener[1] [iD], Kerem Kayabay[2] [iD], and P. Erhan Eren[1] [iD]

[1] Informatics Institute, Middle East Technical University, Ankara, Turkey
{alpbayar,sumut,ereren}@metu.edu.tr
[2] Network Technologies Department, Tübitak Ulakbim, Ankara, Turkey
kerem.kayabay@tubitak.gov.tr

Abstract. The Industrial Internet of Things (IIoT) covers many computing devices and sensors constantly generating and exchanging data in a complicated network. Ongoing research tries to fit decentralized edge computing architectures in IIoT environments with urgent computation and action requirements. This paper investigates state-of-the-art edge computing applications based on security, latency, resource utilization, and energy efficiency aspects as well as application domains. Accordingly, a set of case studies for researchers and practitioners to explore or develop applications of edge structures in industrial environments are presented. It is identified that socio-technical issues related to organizations going through digital transformation can point to a possible future research area.

Keywords: Edge Computing · Internet of Things · Industrial IoT · Industrial Use Cases

1 Introduction

Internet of things (IoT) is a term coined by Kevin Ashton in 1999, enabling objects to manage their tasks without human intervention through the data gathered from their sensors and actuators. Industrial IoT (IIoT) refers to IoT applications in industrial domains [1]. IIoT data are traditionally sent and processed in cloud-based central computing architectures. As the volume and velocity of data increase, transmitting all the data to a central cloud for processing becomes costly in terms of time and network resources. Gartner predicts that around 75% of business data will be generated outside a traditional central cloud architecture by 2025. This number was around 10% in 2021 [2]. In critical IIoT environments where a business decision requires immediate computation and action, edge computing as a new paradigm brings faster response times. It reduces network congestion by moving computing and storage near where data is generated.

Edge computing is a paradigm where computations occur closer to the data source. The term edge refers to the node in the opposite direction of the cloud data center [2]. Fog computing is a similar concept introduced by Cisco, focusing more on the infrastructure between edge devices and central cloud servers [3]. Fog and Edge terms are used interchangeably in this study because they try to achieve the same from the perspective

J. Á. Bañares et al. (Eds.): GECON 2022, LNCS 13430, pp. 124–131, 2023.
https://doi.org/10.1007/978-3-031-29315-3_11

of business objectives. Investigating available real-life applications and understanding the edge architectures is significant for organizations since practitioners can understand the technology trends and architectures for a particular IIoT edge computing use case. While paradigms such as edge computing emerge, there is a research gap in related work [3–7] on guiding digitally transforming organizations to utilize them strategically. These studies review existing edge architectures, possible application domains, and objectives; however, they lack a business strategy perspective. Accordingly, the research questions of the study are formed:

- What kind of real-life applications of edge computing and case studies are used in the industry regarding an IIoT environment?
- What are the main objectives of real-life edge computing applications?
- How do these objectives shape edge computing technology trends and architectures?

This paper investigates applications of edge architectures in the industry and groups them according to their objectives and application areas. It aims to present the current implementation status of edge technologies and trends to assist organizations in reaching their business objectives. The paper is structured as follows: Sect. 2 presents the motivation, challenges behind using edge computing in IIoT, and market trends. The literature review methodology is explained in Sect. 3, while Sect. 4 presents the real-life applications and case studies. Lastly, discussion and conclusion are stated.

2   Edge Computing in IIoT

This paper groups edge computing studies in IIoT according to four main objectives: **latency, security, energy efficiency**, and **resource utilization**. **Latency** is a common concern between edge applications. In an experiment [8] on a face recognition task, it has been shown that moving applications from the cloud to the edge reduces 900 to 160 ms. in response time. With less latency, edge nodes can help monitor and control processes [9] or machine status [10], make forecasts under uncertainty [11]. Edge computing platforms are heterogeneous considering data communication, protocols, policies, platforms, and energy consumption, and these differences result in interoperability challenges [5]. Using computationally less complex heterogeneous devices at the edge brings vulnerabilities regarding privacy and **security** in the network [12], which is the second objective the literature focuses on. For efficiently managing these platforms, there are solutions to increase flexibility, scalability, and availability of edge devices stated as **resource utilization** objectives. Finally, **energy efficiency** is a vital aspect to consider in edge architecture s while utilizing edge nodes, referring to the energy consumption of edge devices [13]. Report in [14] identifies deployment strategies as full edge provider, partner edge provider, aggregator edge provider, and limited edge provider [14]. Knowing these roles and strategies in the market is essential to achieve business goals and forming an edge computing adoption strategy.

3   Research Method

This study has been structured based on Kitchenham's guidelines [15] in order to find case studies and real-life examples of edge computing applications regarding IIoT environments. Snowballing approach is combined with a database search. The following keywords are determined as a starting point of the search: "Edge," "Fog," "Computing," "Industrial," and "IoT." Web of Science and IEEE Explore are selected for search databases. Search results are stored in MS Excel. 67 initial results were found after searching the Web of Science Core Collection. Only four of them were released before 2017, and the number of published papers had increased by the year of 2021. 15 studies were selected after the initial elimination. After fully reading these articles, and including references of the references of those studies, 28 papers were selected as **Primary Studies** (PS). The studies focusing on edge computing use cases, applications, and architectures in IIoT, covering on algorithms, tools, benefits, and implementation challenges were regarded as PS, and 16 of them are journal articles, while 11 studies are conference papers, and one is a book chapter. Authors conducted iterative meetings for identifying main objectives and trends for grouping papers. Domain-specific IoT articles with no edge computing implementation were excluded from the search. Studies targeting domains other than manufacturing such as smart cities, autonomous driving, and healthcare, were excluded. The papers that include technical solutions were included if they explain a particular case study application in IIoT domain.

4   Case Studies and Applications

This section reviews applications of edge architectures in the industry and groups them according to objective and application areas. Studies are explained regarding how the architectures and trends are shaped to fulfill the objectives, allowing practitioners to have an idea while developing implementations for their cases. Studies focusing on security, latency, resource utilization, and energy efficiency are presented in Table 1. Objectives are shown in **bold,** while trends are shown in *italic*.

There are many studies related to *blockchain* and edge computing convergence in the literature concerning the **security** of IIoT systems, such as [12, 24, 31]. An approach that uses blockchain and context-aware security for IIoT environments was proposed in [17], and implementation in an additive manufacturing site was presented. When data is provided with blockchain instead of cloud, it reduces communication costs and increases bandwidth efficiency. [16] integrates blockchain for increasing security in an agroindustry platform to monitor and support decisions in a dairy farm. ZigBee was used to connect IoT gateways and sensors and a Raspberry Pi as edge node for preprocessing IoT data and forwarding it to the cloud. A data processing framework is proposed in [25], enabling secure data storage using edge in IIoT systems. Data management and encryption challenges are summarized, and solutions proposed were evaluated using simulations in a prototype to monitor the temperature in a factory. [18] implemented security application in a simulated smart factory to observe the effectiveness under cyber security scenarios. An edge computing smart grid architecture has been proposed in [27], where data load balancing can be achieved with low **latency** and increased **security**.

Table 1. Papers are grouped by their objective and applications

Papers	Main Objective	Application Domain
[16]	Security	Agricultural Monitoring
[17]	Security	Additive Manufacturing
[18]	Security	Simulated Factory
[19]	Resource Utilization	Real-Time Gas Pressure Control
[20]	Resource Utilization	Predictive Maintenance
[7]	Latency + Energy Efficiency	Active Maintenance
[13]	Latency + Energy Efficiency	Software Defined Network
[21]	Energy Efficiency + Resource Utilization	Air Quality Monitoring
[22]	Energy Efficiency + Resource Utilization	Smart Manufacturing System
[6]	Security + Latency	Active Maintenance
[23]	Security + Latency	Smart Grid
[24]	Security + Latency	Simulation
[25]	Security + Resource Utilization	Factory Temperature Monitoring
[26]	Latency + Security + Resource Utilization	Conveyor Routing, Distributed Predictive Maintenance
[27]	Latency + Resource Utilization	Simulation with real IIoT Data
[28]	Security + Resource Utilization	Real-Time Machine Data Analytics
[29]	Latency + Resource Utilization	Image Classification Simulation
[30]	Latency + Resource Utilization	Real-Time Anomaly Detection
[31]	Latency + Resource Utilization	Numerical Experiments
[32]	Latency + Resource Utilization	Vertical Plant Wall System
[33]	Latency + Resource Utilization	Industrial Robotics
[34]	Latency + Resource Utilization + Energy Efficiency	Smart Manufacturing

Energy efficiency and **resource utilization** in terms of computational workload are vital aspects to consider while utilizing edge nodes. *Software Defined Networking* is widely used for managing a network of middleware devices, as reviewed in [13], where the trade-off between energy efficiency and **latency** is evaluated. [35] proposes a technical architecture that leverages SDN with Network Function Virtualization (NFV) and serverless architectures to reduce the high energy consumption of edge architectures. An adaptive data transmission algorithm using SDN in edge computing for IIoT is proposed in [34] to find an optimal route for traffic load, task deadlines, and energy consumption. To achieve an industrial internet, [22] proposed a framework consisting of high-level embedded microcontrollers and gateway systems. With the help of distributed computing, the gateway efficiently performs network management, data collection, and communication, considering power consumption and providing better **scalability** than traditional IIoT solutions. A similar problem is addressed in [27], which obtains optimized scheduling of IIoT data according to priorities. [7] proposes an architecture to resolve latency and boost energy efficiency in manufacturing utilizes SDN in the network domain. In the proposed architecture, application domain provides monitoring and control services; data domain provides data cleaning and feature extraction using Hadoop; and the network domain utilizes SDN and Time Sensitive Networking (TSN) to manage devices such as Raspberry Pi connected with OPC UA. This edge architecture is compared to the existing private cloud on a candy packaging production line in terms of productivity [6]. Although the network's speed decreased from 16MB/s to 6 MB/s after switching to edge, the results show that edge provides more productivity in high volume mass production. To monitor the real-time status of machinery and conduct predictive maintenance, a database is created in [20], small enough to fit in memories of edge devices using Python SQLite.

Containerized edge architectures are evaluated in [32] regarding industrial requirements, measuring round trip time, bandwidth, processing capabilities, and **latency** while doing machine learning tasks for predictive maintenance. Microsoft Azure IoT Edge is utilized for running container applications on Raspberry Pi. Results show that containerization does not decrease performance while **increasing flexibility and scalability**. A manufacturing process control system has been proposed in [36] to monitor production lines and collect and analyze data to increase efficiency. Stream data were collected from sensors through communication adapters working on OPC UA and MTConnect protocols. Edge node, streaming data in real-time, provides control signals. [21] implemented an air quality monitoring system using data from Arduino sensors spread across a university campus. Low Power Wide Area Network (LoRA) gets data from sensors, transmits data to the LoRa gateway, then to an edge gateway of Kubernetes minion installed on a Raspberry Pi for final unified delivery to the data center. MQTT protocol enables sending alerts to devices if there are anomalies in the data. An open-source architecture for industrial networks called IFog4.0 is proposed in [19] with case studies in an emulated gas regulation station environment. A Fog-Management module has been developed to manage Docker containers. Fog Computing Platform reference architecture is proposed for IIoT applications in [26], using open standards, OPC UA and TSN. A machine is provided with packages containing tags, and the system delivers them to the destination by accessing a database through reading the tag. Network configurations and the benefits of using an edge architecture in different use cases of the same architecture are explained in detail in [37]. Similar fog-based industrial robotic systems are proposed in [33] and [28].

Utilizing *deep learning* requires high computation power and bandwidth. In an edge architecture tailored for deep learning [29], complexity is optimized in line with the computational capacity of edge devices. To evaluate the solution, authors formed a convolutional neural network using real-world IIoT data. They applied experiments that reduce network traffic while maintaining the model's classification accuracy in an object identification task of 30 different components. One way of processing deep learning in the edge is by inferencing, executing pre-trained models with newly generated visual content from mobile edge devices. [38] formulated the inference offloading problem to **minimize energy consumption** and evaluated the performance using simulations. In order to use deep learning for anomaly detection, performance of different architectures are tested in [30]. Trade-off of choosing the architecture considering scalability, bandwidth, and delay have been presented. The author concludes that scaling cloud computation power results in full cloud outperforming the edge.

5   Discussion and Conclusion

In this study, a comprehensive literature review was conducted for edge computing architecture and applications to business cases in IIoT. The main contributions of this paper are stated as follows: (I) Explanations of case studies retrieved from the literature are provided as guidance for organizations and (II) Different application domains are investigated regarding security, latency, resource utilization, and energy efficiency objectives. Additionally, trends, motivation, and implementation challenges of edge computing are explained for both researchers and professionals. Furthermore, this study presents tailored approaches for effective resource utilization in terms of efficient computation needs of the businesses such as complex deep learning applications or simpler monitoring tasks. Although there are plenty of studies focusing on when and why to implement edge architectures, all example applications are experimental. The main research highlights are explained as below:

- While integrating different approaches, there is a trade-off between increasing security, reducing latency, increasing energy consumption, and making the network more complex with potential interoperability problems [24]. For example, deploying blockchain to increase security results in more energy consumption.
- Further trends of edge computing are identified: Blockchain has been incorporated into IIoT networks for security. Approaches such as SDN, containerization, and offloading algorithms are used to increase resource utilization and energy efficiency.

There are some limitations of this study. First, snowballing may have reduced the reproducibility of the search process, and it is likely to obtain further examples. Secondly, a limited number of non-academic resources, such as reports of institutes or consulting agencies, have been reviewed to present trends in edge computing. Also, grouping papers by their objectives and identified trends may contain subjectivity.

Findings show that there is no framework or guidance for selecting and implementing an appropriate edge computing architecture. In future work, we plan to investigate technology management approaches to bridge the socio-technical knowledge gaps in the literature.

References

1. What is the Internet of Things (IoT)? https://www.oracle.com/tr/internet-of-things/what-is-iot/. Accessed 20 Dec 2021
2. What edge computing means for infrastructure and operations leaders. https://www.gartner.com/smarterwithgartner/what-edge-computing-means-for-infrastructure-and-operations-leaders. Accessed 20 Dec 2021

3. Qiu, T., Chi, J., Zhou, X., Ning, Z., Atiquzzaman, M., Wu, D.O.: Edge computing in industrial internet of things: architecture, advances and challenges. IEEE Commun. Surv. Tutorials **22**, 2462–2488 (2020)

4. Yu, W., et al.: A survey on the edge computing for the internet of things. IEEE Access. **6**, 6900–6919 (2018)

5. Khan, W., Ahmed, E., Hakak, S., Yaqoob, I., Ahmed, A.: Edge computing: a survey. Future Gener. Comput. Syst. **97**, 219–235 (2019)

6. Chen, B., Wan, J., Celesti, A., Li, D., Abbas, H., Zhang, Q.: Edge computing in IoT-based manufacturing. IEEE Commun. Mag. **56**, 103–109 (2018)

7. Chalapathi, G.S.S., Chamola, V., Vaish, A., Buyya, R.: Fog/Edge Computing For Security, Privacy, and Applications, pp. 293–325. Springer, Cham (2021)

8. Yi, S., Hao, Z., Qin, Z., Li, Q.: Fog computing: platform and applications. In: 3rd IEEE Workshop on Hot Topics in Web Systems and Technologies (HotWeb), Washington DC, USA, pp. 73–78 (2015)

9. Li, L., Ota, K., Dong, M.: Deep learning for smart industry: efficient manufacture inspection system with fog computing. IEEE Trans. Industr. Inf. **14**, 4665–4673 (2018)

10. Bose, S.K., Kar, B., Roy, M., Gopalakrishnan, P.K., Basu, A.: ADEPOS: anomaly detection based power saving for predictive maintenance using edge computing. In: Proceedings of the 24th Asia and South Pacific Design Automation Conference, pp. 597–602. ACM, Tokyo (2019)

11. Taïk, A., Cherkaoui, S.: Electrical load forecasting using edge computing and federated learning. In: ICC 2020 - 2020 IEEE International Conference on Communications (ICC), Dublin, Ireland, pp. 1–6 (2020)

12. Wu, Y., Dai, H.-N., Wang, H.: Convergence of blockchain and edge computing for secure and scalable IIot critical infrastructures in industry 4.0. IEEE Internet Things J. **8**, 2300–2317 (2021)

13. Kaur, K., Garg, S., Aujla, G.S., Kumar, N., Rodrigues, J.J.P.C., Guizani, M.: Edge computing in the industrial internet of things environment: software-defined-networks-based edge-cloud interplay. IEEE Commun. Mag. **56**, 44–51 (2018)

14. Brava, C., Backström, H.: Whitepaper on edge computing deployment strategies. https://www.ericsson.com/en/reports-and-papers/white-papers/edge-computing-and-deployment-strategies-for-communication-service-providers. Accessed 20 Dec 2021

15. Kitchenham, B.: Procedures for performing systematic reviews. Keele, UK, **33** (2004)

16. Sittón-Candanedo, I., Alonso, R.S., Corchado, J.M., Rodríguez-González, S., Casado-Vara, R.: A review of edge computing reference architectures and a new global edge proposal. Futur. Gener. Comput. Syst. **99**, 278–294 (2019)

17. Portal, G., de Matos, E., Hessel, F.: An edge decentralized security architecture for industrial IoT applications. In: IEEE 6th World Forum on Internet of Things (WF-IoT), New Orleans, USA, pp. 1–6 (2020)

18. Güven, E.Y., Çamurcu, A.Y.: Edge computing security application: Kılıç. In: 3rd International Conference on Computer Science and Engineering (UBMK), Sarajevo, Bosnia and Herzegovina, pp. 248–253 (2018)

19. Ghazi Vakili, M., Demartini, C., Guerrera, M., Montrucchio, B.: Open source fog architecture for industrial IoT automation based on industrial protocols. In: IEEE 43rd Annual Computer Software and Applications Conference (COMPSAC), Milwaukee, WI, USA, pp. 570–578 (2019)

20. Oyekanlu, E.: Predictive edge computing for time series of industrial IoT and large scale critical infrastructure based on open-source software analytic of big data. In: IEEE International Conference on Big Data (Big Data), Boston, MA, USA, pp. 1663–1669 (2017)

21. Kristiani, E., Yang, C.-T., Huang, C.-Y., Wang, Y.-T., Ko, P.-C.: The implementation of a cloud-edge computing architecture using OpenStack and Kubernetes for air quality monitoring application. Mobile Netw. Appl. **26**(3), 1070–1092 (2020). https://doi.org/10.1007/s11036-020-01620-5

22. Chen, C.-H., Lin, M.-Y., Liu, C.-C.: Edge Computing gateway of the industrial internet of things using multiple collaborative microcontrollers. IEEE Network **32**, 24–32 (2018)

23. Okay, F.Y., Ozdemir, S.: A fog computing based smart grid model. In: International Symposium on Networks, Computers and Communications (ISNCC), Yasmine Hammamet, Tunisia, pp. 1–6 (2016)

24. Kumar, T., et al.: BlockEdge: blockchain-edge framework for industrial IoT networks. IEEE Access. **8**, 154166–154185 (2020)

25. Fu, J.-S., Liu, Y., Chao, H.-C., Bhargava, B.K., Zhang, Z.-J.: Secure data storage and searching for industrial IoT by integrating fog computing and cloud computing. IEEE Trans. Industr. Inf. **14**, 4519–4528 (2018)

26. Pop, P., et al.: The FORA fog computing platform for industrial IoT. Inf. Syst. **98**, 101727 (2021)

27. Chekired, D.A., Khoukhi, L., Mouftah, H.T.: Industrial IoT data scheduling based on hierarchical fog computing: a key for enabling smart factory. IEEE Trans. Industr. Inf. **14**, 4590–4602 (2018)

28. Denzler, P., Ruh, J., Kadar, M., Avasalcai, C., Kastner, W.: Towards consolidating industrial use cases on a common fog computing platform. In: 25th IEEE International Conference on Emerging Technologies and Factory Automation (ETFA), Vienna, Austria, pp. 172–179 (2020)

29. Liang, F., Yu, W., Liu, X., Griffith, D., Golmie, N.: Toward edge-based deep learning in industrial internet of things. IEEE Internet Things J. **7**, 4329–4341 (2020)

30. Ferrari, P., et al.: Performance evaluation of full-cloud and edge-cloud architectures for Industrial IoT anomaly detection based on deep learning. In: II Workshop on Metrology for Industry 4.0 and IoT (MetroInd4.0 IoT), Naples, Italy, pp. 420–425 (2019)

31. Lee, C.K.M., Huo, Y.Z., Zhang, S.Z., Ng, K.K.H.: Design of a smart manufacturing system with the application of multi-access edge computing and blockchain technology. IEEE Access. **8**, 28659–28667 (2020). https://doi.org/10.1109/ACCESS.2020.2972284

32. Liu, Y., Lan, D., Pang, Z., Karlsson, M., Gong, S.: Performance evaluation of containerization in edge-cloud computing stacks for industrial applications: a client perspective. IEEE Open J. Ind. Electron. Soc. **2**, 153–168 (2021)

33. Shaik, M.S., et al.: Enabling fog-based industrial robotics systems. In: 25th IEEE International Conference on Emerging Technologies and Factory Automation (ETFA), Vienna, Austria, pp. 61–68 (2020)

34. Li, X., Li, D., Wan, J., Liu, C., Imran, M.: Adaptive transmission optimization in SDN-based industrial internet of things with edge computing. IEEE Internet Things J. **5**, 1351–1360 (2018)

35. Djemame, K.: Energy efficiency in edge environments: a serverless computing approach. In: Tserpes, K., et al. (eds.) Economics of Grids, Clouds, Systems, and Services, pp. 181–184. Springer International Publishing, Cham (2021). https://doi.org/10.1007/978-3-030-92916-9_15

36. Wu, D., et al.: A fog computing-based framework for process monitoring and prognosis in cyber-manufacturing. J. Manuf. Syst. **43**, 25–34 (2017)

37. Barzegaran, M., et al.: Fogification of electric drives: an industrial use case. In: 25th IEEE International Conference on Emerging Technologies and Factory Automation (ETFA), Vienna, Austria, pp. 77–84 (2020)

38. Xu, Z., et al.: Energy-aware inference offloading for DNN-driven applications in mobile edge clouds. IEEE Trans. Parallel Distrib. Syst. **32**, 799–814 (2021)

A Black-Box Graph Partitioner for Generalized Deep Neural Network Parallelization

Jaume Mateu Cuadrat(ID), Daon Park(ID), and Bernhard Egger(✉)(ID)

Seoul National University, Seoul, Republic of Korea
{jaume,daon,bernhard}@csap.snu.ac.kr

Abstract. In the quest for higher accuracy, large deep neural networks (DNNs) have grown significantly over the past few years. Training and executing large networks with trillions of parameters requires high-end hardware that is expensive to own or rent. A more economical alternative is to distribute the workload to several less powerful but cheaper machines. To devise an efficient workload division, existing parallelization strategies require users to posses intricate knowledge of the model, available hardware, and algorithms. In this paper, we present BBGraP, a device- and model-agnostic black-box partitioner that computes efficient parallelization plans for deep learning inference. For a given network and hardware configuration, BBGraP generates a data-parallel execution plan for each machine. The initial workload partition is optimized by eliminating redundant operations, data transfers, and synchronization points. As a proof-of-concept, BBGraP is applied to a set comprising three distributed nodes and achieves a 30% reduced latency compared to a single node.

Keywords: Deep Learning · Inference Parallelization · Resource Scheduling

1 Introduction

Deep neural networks (DNNs) are now ubiquitously adopted in many domains [1,6, 13]. Recent large DNNs, such as the autoregressive language model GPT-3, achieve impressive performance, however, providing the necessary hardware resources to train and run such large models with trillions of parameters has become a challenge [4].

An established alternative to owning hardware is cloud computing. Cloud computing allows businesses to add and remove resources on demand [3]; however, the high-end servers required to train and execute large DNNs are expensive to rent [2]. A more economical alternative is to distribute the workload to several, but less powerful machines that cost only a fraction of high-end servers.

Several techniques distribute a large DNN to a multitude nodes, such as data parallelism [5], model parallelism [9], and intra-layer parallelism [11]. Finding the optimal division is a complex task as the best division depends on the hardware configuration, the number of nodes, and the network [10]. Data parallel workload divisions can split the work along different dimensions, further enlarging the number of possible divisions.

Existing parallelization methods require intricate knowledge of the network and the available hardware to create an efficient work division. In this work, we present

© The Author(s), under exclusive license to Springer Nature Switzerland AG 2023
J. Á. Bañares et al. (Eds.): GECON 2022, LNCS 13430, pp. 132–140, 2023.
https://doi.org/10.1007/978-3-031-29315-3_12

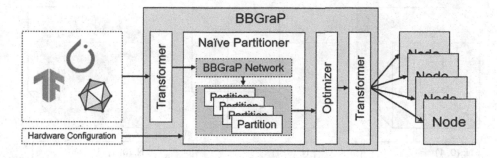

Fig. 1. The BBGraP framework.

BBGraP, a model-and device-agnostic technique to partition and optimize a given DNN workload for a number of heterogeneous nodes. BBGraP distributes a DNN to a variable number of heterogeneous nodes. It first produces an initial distribution and adds the necessary data transfer and synchronization operations. In a second step, a graph optimizer removes unnecessary operators, removes or tailors data transfers, and eliminates synchronization operations that are not required anymore. Initial results show that the parallel workload achieves a 30% lower latency on a three-node configuration compared to a single, more powerful node.

The remainder of this paper is organized as follows. Section 2 discusses the background and related work. Section 3 describes the operation and components of BBGraP. In Sect. 4, we present preliminary results of workload divisions on up to three homogeneous nodes. Section 5, finally, concludes this paper and discusses future work.

2 Background and Related Work

Distributed deep learning techniques employ data parallelism, model parallelism, and intra-layer parallelism. Data parallelism distributes the data to all workers at the expense of sending the full model to all workers and thus increasing memory requirements. Model parallelism distributes the model layer-by-layer which may cause bottlenecks between the worker nodes. Intra-layer parallelism divides operators between the workers which in turn requires synchronization to maintain operator semantics.

Different types of data partitions and workload distributions have been explored in the past. MoDNN [7] divides the network and sends the data via Wi-Fi to different devices. The network is partitioned layer-by-layer, hence, data synchronization is required at the end of each layer. DeepThings [14] focuses on early layers of the network where size of activations exceeds that of the weights. Layers are divided in the height- and width-dimension. DeepThings is aimed at IoT devices and lacks flexibility when it comes to the shapes of the partitions. DeeperThings [12] focuses on fully-connected layers and layers where the size of the weights is significantly larger than that of input activations. This approach is limited to weight and output partitioning, and only supports specific partitionings. DeepThings and DeeperThings outperform MoDNN because they don't require synchronization after each layer; however, both methods lack flexibility in the type of generated partitionings.

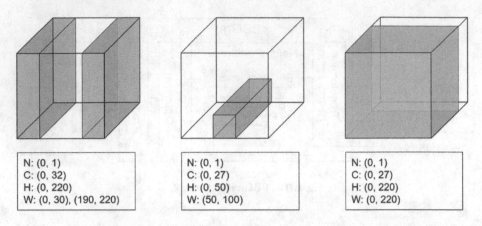

N: (0, 1)
C: (0, 32)
H: (0, 220)
W: (0, 30), (190, 220)

N: (0, 1)
C: (0, 27)
H: (0, 50)
W: (50, 100)

N: (0, 1)
C: (0, 27)
H: (0, 220)
W: (0, 220)

Fig. 2. ShapeMap examples (N: batches, C: channels, H: rows, W: columns).

The CSDF partitioner [8] performs both model and data partition. Similar to MoDNN, only weight and output partitionings are supported that require synchronization after each layer. CSDF focuses on throughput, so not all resources are utilized at all times.

3 BBGraP: A Black-Box DNN Model Partitioner

BBGraP takes a DNN model and a hardware configuration as inputs. After transforming the network into an internal format, an initial workload partition is created. This partition synchronizes all nodes after each layer. In a second step, BBGraP analyzes and optimizes the execution plan for each node by cropping or eliminating unnecessary data transfers and synchronization operations. Figure 1 depicts the organization of BBGraP.

3.1 Transformer

The transformation step converts an existing network into BBGraP's internal *ShapeMap* format. Figure 2 shows a few examples of ShapeMaps partitioned in various dimensions. A ShapeMap can even define intervals with multiple ranges as shown in the first example of Fig. 2. The generated network hierarchy closely resembles the original network and encompasses all required parameters to partition the workload and later regenerate partitioned, stand-alone networks in the original format.

3.2 Partitioner

For the initial partitioning, BBGraP divides each layer into a an evenly distributed workload across all available nodes. The initial partitioning is computed from the last layer to the first using the final output *ShapeMap*. This direction makes it easier to compute the overlaps that occur due to different stride, padding, and dilation parameters. As shown in Eq. 1, the output is equally divided by the number of nodes. Table 1 defines

Table 1. Table of variables used in the equations

Symbol	Description
d	Partitioning direction (c, h, or w)
N_d	Number of nodes assigned to direction d
I / O	Original input / output size
$pI_{(d,i)} / pO_{(d,i)}$	Input/output partition size, partitioned in direction d and assigned to node i
K_d	Kernel size in direction d
tK_d	True kernel size in direction d
D_d, S_d, IV_d	Dilation, stride, and interval in direction d
$P_{(d_0,d_1)}$	Padding size in direction of d_0 (h or w) and d_1 (left or right)

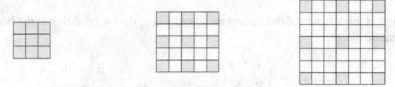

(a) 3×3 kernel with dilation 1.   (b) 3×3 kernel with dilation 2.   (c) 3×3 kernel with dilation 3.

Fig. 3. 3×3 kernels with different dilation values.

the variables used in the equations. The remainder of the integer division O/N_d is distributed to the nodes in a round-robin manner. For example, an 8×8 output feature map partitioned to three nodes in width direction results the partitions $pO_{(w,0)} = 3 \times 8$, $pO_{(w,1)} = 3 \times 8$, and $pO_{(w,2)} = 2 \times 8$.

$$pO_{(d,i)} = \lfloor O/N_d \rfloor \tag{1}$$

Once the output dimensions are known, BBGraP computes the input division by taking the kernel size, dilation, stride, and padding into account. First, the true kernel size is realized with Eq. 2. A kernel with a dilation $D = 1$ is the kernel itself, but for dilation values larger than 1, the kernel is spread out as illustrated in Fig. 3.

$$tK_d = (K_d - 1) \cdot D_d + 1 \tag{2}$$

Using the true kernel size, the size of the input is given by Eq. 3; Fig. 4 illustrates the calculation of the input partition for an output of $3(1 \times 1)$ and a 3×3 kernel with dilation and stride of 2.

$$IV_{(d,i)} = (O - 1) \cdot S_d + tK_d \tag{3}$$

The start and end index of the input data partition for node i are given by Eqs. 4 and 5. $P_{(d,0)}$ denotes the padding in either width-left or height-left, and $P_{(d,1)}$ denotes the padding in either width-right or height-right direction. For example, $P_{(w,0)}$ refers to

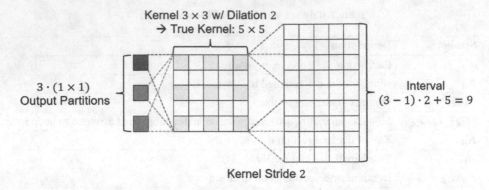

Fig. 4. Example of calculating input interval size.

padding at the left side of the feature map, and $P_{(h,1)}$ denotes padding at the bottom of the feature map.

$$\text{Left}_{(d,i)} = \begin{cases} 0 & \text{if } i = 0, \\ S_d \cdot \sum_{j=0}^{i-1} pO_{(d,j)} - P_{(d,0)} & \text{otherwise.} \end{cases} \quad (4)$$

$$\text{Right}_{(d,i)} = \begin{cases} IV_{(d,i)} + \text{Left}_{(d,i)} - P_{(d,0)} & \text{if } i = 0, \\ IV_{(d,i)} + \text{Left}_{(d,i)} - P_{(d,1)} & \text{if } i = N_d - 1, \\ IV_{(d,i)} + \text{Left}_{(d,i)} & \text{otherwise.} \end{cases} \quad (5)$$

The input partitioned in direction d for node i is given by Eq. 6.

$$pI_{(d,i)} = [\text{Left}_{(d,i)}, \text{Right}_{(d,i)}] \quad (6)$$

Once all partitions have been created, BBGraP inserts concatenation and crop operators after each layer to join the outputs and prepare the inputs for the next layer.

3.3 Graph Optimizer

The initial partitioning creates a full copy of the output data at each node. This introduces many unnecessary data transfer, synchronization, and crop operators, depending on which parts of the previous layer's output are required as inputs to the following layer. The graph optimizer analyzes the available output and required input data for each node and removes unnecessary operators. As illustrated in Fig. 5, there are four distinct cases (b)–(e). Figure 5 (a) shows the initial partitioning with output α of layer $l-1$, the full activations β and the required input γ for layer l.

1. **Input bigger than output**, Fig. 5(b): the missing data is fetched from device node 1 and concatenated on device node 2.
2. **Input identical to output**, Fig. 5(c): no data dependencies exist, and crop and concatenation operators are deleted.

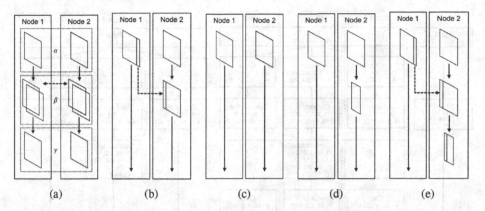

Fig. 5. Graph optimizations: 5a shows the initial state prior to optimization. 5b–5e illustrate the optimization process in dependence of the dimensions of the output and next layer's input.

3. **Input smaller than output**, Fig. 5(d–e): if the generated output is larger than the required input on the same node, in most cases, no data dependencies exist and a crop operator is used to reduce the input data to the expected size. It is, however, possible that a data dependency still exists; in that case, the optimizer adjusts the data transfer and crop operator to make sure the necessary data is fetched before the computation continues on device node 2.

4   Evaluation

4.1   Graph Partitioning and Optimization

Figure 6 illustrates the operation of BBGraP on a small toy network. Figure 6(a) shows the initial network comprising two convolutional layers. The initial partition to three nodes with data transfer operations (crop and concatenate) is shown in Fig. 6(b); data dependencies are shown in red. The graph optimizer is able to remove unnecessary data transfer and synchronizations for nodes 1 and 3 since the size of the first convolution's output is identical to the required input for the second convolution as illustrated by Fig. 6(c).

4.2   Latency of Parallel Inference

For a preliminary evaluation of BBGraP, we compare the performance of single-node inference with parallelized workloads to two and three homogeneous nodes. The parallelized network is ResNet50; each node is equipped with an Intel i5-10400 6-core/12-thread processor and sufficient memory. The network operators are executed using Intel's oneDNN library; data transfers and synchronizations orchestrated by a small custom runtime. Due to limitations of the runtime, BBGraP was artificially limited to output channel division.

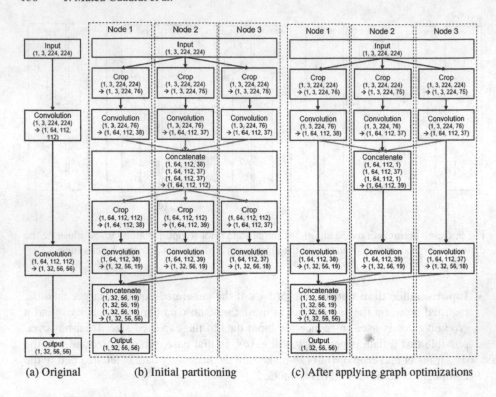

(a) Original (b) Initial partitioning (c) After applying graph optimizations

Fig. 6. Original, initial, and optimized graph. Red arrows denote data dependencies/synchronization points between the nodes. (Color figure online)

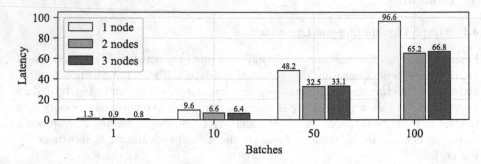

Fig. 7. Latency of ResNet50 inference on 1–3 nodes.

Figure 7 plots the interference latency of ResNet50 for a batch size of 1, 10, 50, and 100 on one to three nodes. We observe that using two nodes reduces the latency significantly. With three nodes, however, latency does not improve anymore. The culprit is the non-scalable output channel division that requires full synchronization of all output data to all nodes after each convolution. We even observe a small increase in latency for larger batch sizes; this is because our communication library does not use broadcast but transfers the output of one node to all other nodes in a serial manner.

5   Conclusion and Future Work

This paper has presented our ongoing work on BBGraP, a device-and model-agnostic framework that computes an efficient workload division for DNN inference. While the framework still has many shortcomings, the results show the potential of the presented approach.

At the moment, BBGraP only supports homogeneous nodes and both the initial partition, the graph optimization, and the runtime to orchestrate execution on multiple nodes still offer lots of room for improvements. Our ongoing and future work on BBGraP includes support for heterogeneous nodes by providing the computational and memory resources as an input. The graph optimizer is being improved to also consider layer fusion; the large number of potential workload divisions in multiple directions and fused layers will require clever search space pruning to keep the search time reasonable. Finally, we are also working on improving BBGraP's runtime to transfer data more efficiently between nodes, particularly, for scenarios with many nodes.

Acknowledgments. We thank the anonymous reviewers for their helpful feedback and suggestions. This work was funded, in parts, by the Korean National Research Foundation by grants 2022R1F1A1074967, 21A20151113068 (BK21 Plus for Pioneers in Innovative Computing - Dept. of Computer Science & Engineering, SNU), 10077609 (MOTIE/KEIT), and the Samsung Advanced Institute of Technology. ICT at Seoul National University provided research facilities for this study.

References

1. Ahmedt-Aristizabal, D., Armin, M.A., Denman, S., Fookes, C., Petersson, L.: Graph-based deep learning for medical diagnosis and analysis: past, present and future. Sensors **21**(14), 4758 (2021)
2. Amazon: Amazon ec2 p4 instances: highest performance for ml training and HPC applications in the cloud (2020). https://aws.amazon.com/ec2/instance-types/p4/
3. Buyya, R., Yeo, C.S., Venugopal, S., Broberg, J., Brandic, I.: Cloud computing and emerging it platforms: vision, hype, and reality for delivering computing as the 5th utility. Futur. Gener. Comput. Syst. **25**(6), 599–616 (2009)
4. Fedus, W., Zoph, B., Shazeer, N.: Switch transformers: scaling to trillion parameter models with simple and efficient sparsity (2021)
5. Krizhevsky, A., Sutskever, I., Hinton, G.E.: Imagenet classification with deep convolutional neural networks. In: Advances in Neural Information Processing Systems, vol. 25 (2012)
6. Lee, W., Seong, J.J., Ozlu, B., Shim, B.S., Marakhimov, A., Lee, S.: Biosignal sensors and deep learning-based speech recognition: a review. Sensors **21**(4), 1399 (2021)
7. Mao, J., Chen, X., Nixon, K.W., Krieger, C., Chen, Y.: Modnn: local distributed mobile computing system for deep neural network. In: Design, Automation & Test in Europe Conference & Exhibition (DATE), 2017, pp. 1396–1401. IEEE (2017)
8. Minakova, S., Tang, E., Stefanov, T.: Combining task-and data-level parallelism for high-throughput CNN inference on embedded CPUs-GPUs MPSoCs. In: Orailoglu, A., Jung, M., Reichenbach, M. (eds.) SAMOS 2020. LNCS, vol. 12471, pp. 18–35. Springer, Cham (2020). https://doi.org/10.1007/978-3-030-60939-9_2
9. Narayanan, D., et al.: Pipedream: generalized pipeline parallelism for DNN training. In: Proceedings of the 27th ACM Symposium on Operating Systems Principles, pp. 1–15 (2019)

10. Narayanan, D., et al.: Efficient large-scale language model training on GPU clusters using megatron-lm. In: Proceedings of the International Conference for High Performance Computing, Networking, Storage and Analysis, pp. 1–15 (2021)
11. Shoeybi, M., Patwary, M., Puri, R., LeGresley, P., Casper, J., Catanzaro, B.: Megatron-lm: training multi-billion parameter language models using model parallelism. arXiv preprint. arXiv:1909.08053 (2019)
12. Stahl, R., Hoffman, A., Mueller-Gritschneder, D., Gerstlauer, A., Schlichtmann, U.: Deeperthings: fully distributed CNN inference on resource-constrained edge devices. Int. J. Parallel Prog. 49(4), 600–624 (2021)
13. Sun, F., Liu, J., Wu, J., Pei, C., Lin, X., Ou, W., Jiang, P.: Bert4rec: sequential recommendation with bidirectional encoder representations from transformer. In: Proceedings of the 28th ACM International Conference on Information and Knowledge Management, pp. 1441–1450 (2019)
14. Zhao, Z., Barijough, K.M., Gerstlauer, A.: Deepthings: distributed adaptive deep learning inference on resource-constrained IoT edge clusters. IEEE Trans. Comput. Aided Des. Integr. Circuits Syst. 37(11), 2348–2359 (2018)

New Idea Papers

Selective Data Migration Between Locality Groups in NUMA Systems

Junsung Yook and Bernhard Egger[✉]

Seoul National University, Seoul, Republic of Korea
{junsung,bernhard}@csap.snu.ac.kr

Abstract. Non-uniform memory access (NUMA) architectures exhibit variable memory access latencies that depend on the issuing core and the accessed memory location. To minimize an application's memory access time, the accessed data should be kept as close to the computation as possible. An promising strategy is to deploy groups of threads that access the same data on neighboring cores and close to the accessed data. This not only minimizes remote memory accesses latency but also reduces the amount of accessed cache lines and the traffic incurred by the cache coherence protocol; however, finding and maintaining a good thread group allocation is difficult. This paper presents a novel at-runtime technique that improves application performance through better data locality without prior profiling runs. The presented technique accurately detects accessed memory sections through low-overhead sampling. Sections that are frequently accessed on a remote node are migrated to the local memory node. Migration of unused data such as data streams is avoided by only copying sections that are expected to yield a positive net gain.

Keywords: NUMA(Non-Uniform Memory Access) Architecture · Data Locality Groups · Performance Monitoring Unit

1 Introduction

The memory systems of computer systems are built around the fact that most programs exhibit temporal and spatial data locality. A hierarchy of memories from small and fast to large and slow provides low access latencies and high throughput by exploiting data locality. To achieve maximum performance, a process' working set should be kept in nearby memories. In parallel applications, several threads form locality groups when they access similar data objects. To support the placement of locality groups, NUMA (Non-Uniform Memory Access) architectures provide information on the organization of the physical memory hierarchy [3]. By harnessing this information, it is possible to not only increase the efficiency of caches through improved data reuse but also to reduce the communication overhead in the interconnection network. In other words, achieving better locality increases cache utilization and reduces the memory access latency.

In NUMA architectures, the data access latency depends on the location of the core that requests the data and the physical location of the data. Unlike in hardware-managed

J. Á. Bañares et al. (Eds.): GECON 2022, LNCS 13430, pp. 143–147, 2023.
https://doi.org/10.1007/978-3-031-29315-3_13

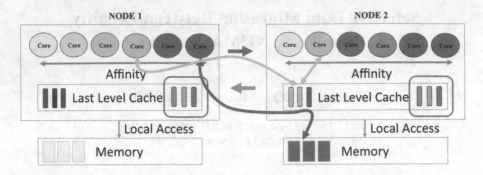

Fig. 1. Illustration of the advantages of local vs. remote memory accesses.

caches, the placement of data pages in memory can be controlled in software; we can thus exploit data locality by placing the accessed data in memory local to the core.

Several studies have proposed techniques to increase data locality to mitigate the cost of remote memory accesses. A common approach is to cluster the threads of an application according to their affinity of shared data [4]. To decide the optimal memory allocation policy, other techniques track memory allocation requests to identify memory objects before profiling the accesses to them [2]. Other approaches aim at preventing congestion in the interconnection network and at the memory controllers by balancing the load and decide the placement of data at runtime [1]. One of the main challenges is to avoid moving data that causes more overhead than benefit. An other difficulty for at-runtime techniques concerns the lack of exact information on memory accesses because they have to rely on sampling to keep the runtime overhead to a minimum. Finally, moving data into local nodes often obstructs load balancing efforts; data should thus be placed in consideration the utilization of memory nodes. All these challenges render low-overhead at-runtime data placement and coordination difficult.

In this paper, we present a technique that can exploit data locality at runtime and with low overhead. A history table is used to identify and migrate only data sections that are expected to yield a net benefit. We employ a technique that is able to infer used or likely-to-be-accessed-next sections of memory objects with a small number of samples and without the need to trace calls to specific routines. Finally, we introduce a placement technique that considers both locality and congestion.

An evaluation on a 72-core Intel NUMA system with 25 real-world programs from three benchmark suites shows that, on average, our migration policy is able to reduce the traffic caused by page movements by 70%. By restoring missing sections of memory objects, it was possible to achieve placements of steady state where threads and data are consistently settled earlier. As a result, the proposed techniques increases application performance by up to 25% and 10% on average over all evaluated parallel programs.

2   Design

The presented technique focuses on (1) relocating processes groups close to their data and (2) balancing the load of requests to the components of the memory subsystem. The thread and data placement is re-evaluated periodically every 100 ms. Memory request events such as the number of L2 cache misses are sampled using the Precise Event-Based Sampling (PEBS) capabilities of the hardware performance monitoring unit.

2.1 Inference of Memory Objects

Sampling every n^{th} cache miss does not reveal the full memory access pattern of a group of threads and, in turn, lead to the identification of several small memory segments that are actually part of a single, larger object. To compensate for missing samples, the presented technique speculatively fills gaps between identified memory segments to capture the entire memory object. The heuristic is based on the idea that the intervals between the addresses of the same memory objects tend to be smaller than those to different memory objects.

The average stride between sampled addresses on the heap segment is obtained by dividing the distance between the largest and smallest address by the number of sampled addresses. If all the intervals between addresses in a sequence of sampled addresses are smaller than the average stride, then the entire range is considered a contiguous region of a memory object. To reduce the computational overhead, the minimal detection unit of a memory region is identical to the size of a physical page or larger.

2.2 Selection of Active Data for Migration

Chunks obtained by inference for sections of memory objects are candidate that can be chosen as active data. In this context, selected chunks represent the working set that are likely to be accessed again in the future, that is active data but not dead data such as data stream. The history table constituted by hash table preserves the previous access history of chunks identified by logical addresses. Through this table, the history of existence of the chunks at each epochs is examined. If the chunk has been accessed previously, the chunk is selected as candidate of migration and a counter which indicates how many times the corresponding chunk have existed is incremented. Or if it is the first time to access, the chunk is first considered as inactive data and it is registered in the history table. Also, chunks that are not accessed within a certain number of epochs are evicted from the history table treating as aged. In addition, the higher the number of times a chunk have existed, which indicated by a corresponding counter, the higher priority is assigned to move it first.

3 Evaluation

We evaluate the presented technique on a 72-core (4-node) Intel Xeon E7-8870 v3 processor with 512 GiB of DRAM. All experiments were performed with NUMA-balancing turned off in the Linux kernel to minimize interference between our technique and the operating system's NUMA balancer. We evaluate 25 benchmarks from the NPB, Parsec and Rodinia benchmark suites.

The results are shown in Fig. 2. The execution time of all benchmarks is normalized to standard execution on Linux. We plot the runtime for data migration with

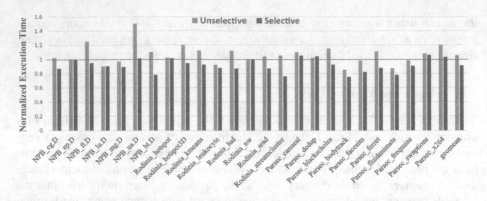

Fig. 2. Comparison of performance with proposed techniques.

(Selective) and without (Unselective) the heuristic to identify memory objects. On average, the presented technique achieves a 10% shorter execution time with individual benchmarks running up to 25% faster. Also noteworthy is the fact that the maximum slowdown for applications that do not profit from the presented technique is consistently below 10% and that all overhead of the presented technique is included in the presented results.

4   Conclusion

This paper has presented a low-overhead, at-runtime approach to data migration for higher performance in NUMA architecture. Objects to be migrated are identified through low-overhead sampling, single, small regions extended into regions through a heuristic. By selecting data objects to be moved based on the likelihood of their reuse, redundant migrations can be avoided. Finally, since localization can destroy the load balance of the memory system and cause congestion that results in performance degradation, our technique balances data across multiple memory nodes.

Experiments with 25 parallel applications show an average performance improvement of 10% and a reduction of the number of data migrations between memory nodes by 70%. For several applications, a 20% or higher performance improvement is obtained, demonstrating that low-overhead data placement techniques are an effective way for significant performance gains on existing hardware.

Acknowledgments. We thank the anonymous reviewers for their helpful feedback and suggestions. This work was funded, in parts, by the Korean National Research Foundation through grants 2022R1F1A1074967 and 21A20151113068 (BK21 Plus for Pioneers in Innovative Computing - Dept. of Computer Science & Engineering, SNU). ICT at Seoul National University provided research facilities for this study.

References

1. Dashti, M., Fedorova, A., Funston, J.: Traffic management: a holistic approach to memory placement on NUMA systems (2012)

2. Lachaize, R., Lepers, B., Quema, V.: Memprof: a memory profiler for NUMA multicore systems. In: 2012 USENIX Annual Technical Conference (USENIX ATC 12), pp. 53–64, Boston, MA. USENIX Association (2012)
3. ORACLE. Memory and thread placement optimization developer's guide (2012)
4. Tam, D., Azimi, R., Stumm, M.: Thread clustering: sharing-aware scheduling on SMP-CMP-SMT multiprocessors (2007)

A Framework to Support Decision-Making Based on AI and Simulation of Large-Scale Models

Unai Arronategui[ID], José Ángel Bañares[(✉)][ID], and José Manuel Colom[ID]

Aragón Institute of Engineering Research (I3A), University of Zaragoza,
Zaragoza, Spain
{unai,banares,jm}@unizar.es

Abstract. Big data collection and analysis is used in industry and public organizations to support decision-making. However, simulation as a core technology to support optimization, or the exploration of large state spaces in artificial intelligence have serious difficulties for industrial adoption. Our approach to solve these difficulties is the adoption of a modelling methodology supported by a cohesive framework based on the Petri net formalism for efficient simulation of complex discrete event systems over large computational infrastructures.

Keywords: Distributed Simulation · Petri Nets · Artificial Intelligence · Decision-making

1 Introduction

The growing interest in large-scale distributed simulations (DS) is motivated by the increasing scale, resolution, and complexity of systems to be studied. Many optimization problems in science and industry involve time-consuming simulations and expensive objective function. The integration of computer simulation with artificial intelligence (AI) is based on the advances in Modelling and Simulation (M&S) and the increase of computational power. However, the scalability of these approaches is limited by the need to fit the model in a computer. Conventional simulation practice on optimization problems typically involves developing a single model and performing simulation experiments in sequence on a single computer. The most common approach is the simplification of the model to fit it to a computer due to the difficulties of transferring it to a distributed simulation using a cluster of computers. Recent work has focused their interest on optimization techniques combined with simulation [3,10,11].

Our approach to solve these difficulties is the adoption of a modelling methodology for efficient simulation of complex discrete event systems (DES) over large computational infrastructures [1,2]. This methodology is supported by a cohesive framework based on the Petri net (PN) formalisms, which collects languages (high level specifications language, code for efficient DS), tools, services (efficient interpreters, compilers, models and scripts to generate code, to automate configuration, deployment and supervision of simulations on premise, public and hybrid clouds with heterogeneous resources), and mechanisms (such as synchronization and dynamic load balancing mechanisms). These mechanisms and tools are the core functionality to support the exploration of large-scale models, requiring strategies implementing different policies to automatize the exploration of large scale space states to support decision-making by the exhaustive exploration and optimization of systems.

DS of large scale DES is a complex problem whose current challenges such as scalability, dynamic configurations, and the integration of different formalisms prevent its adoption by the industry. This work presents the potential of the synergistic integration of AI and simulation.

2 Scalable Compilation, Dynamic Configuration and Federation of Hybrid Simulations

We proposed the integration of AI with the simulation of DES in the context of our developed framework for the M&S of large-scale models. The main characteristic of the previous work has been the adoption of PN as a well-known formalism for modelling complex systems and the proposal of a representation of PNs suitable for efficient distributed simulation. The characteristics of the proposed representation allow facing the most important challenges of the M&S of large systems: scalability, dynamic configuration and interoperability [2].

Instead of the direct emulation of high-level conceptual models, we transform the original structured model into a flat Place/Transition net model. Then, the compilation stage transforms a flat Place/Transition net into an efficient representation for DS. The model compilation bottleneck is the size of code generated limited by the memory of the computer. Scaling the size of the models in a DS requires the generation of large-scale models of arbitrary structure [4], and *modular compilations* based on components that can be compiled separately, deployed at different nodes, and linked with other distributed components. With DS of large-scale systems being complex, configuration management can be a delicate undertaking to implement.

Dynamic configuration of DS is also essential to modify a simulation while it is running. The high coupling of code partitions to be simulated requires that deployment of the code on the execution infrastructure must be sensitive to the model complexity, communications with neighbouring nodes, heterogeneous resource physical characteristics such as processor speed, and the evolution of simulation.

Finally, the complexity of the system must be faced by combining different formalisms to represent all the aspects involved. The adoption of standards such as the High Level Architecture (HLA) solves this problem from the point of view of data interoperability. However, the integration of discrete event simulators with other formalisms, such as continuous specifications, remains a challenge. The compilation of PN specifications produces an event dependency network. This representation supports the production and consumption of events, and facilitates the integration of components in an event-driven architecture.

3   Artificial Intelligence and Simulation

AI today provides a set of mechanisms and tools than can be integrated into the simulation of DES of huge dimensions and intricate structure. The motivation is twofold: On the one hand, searching is an integral part of AI, and a search problem requires the modelling of the problem as a DES. Therefore, for complex systems, AI is faced with the modelling and exploration of large state spaces. On the other hand, the model partition for a DS is a complex optimization problem. Heuristic such as simulating annealing, or genetic algorithms have been proposed to define an initial partition, and reinforcement learning for a dynamic partition considering the evolutionary nature of the simulation [9].

Search is an integral and ubiquitous part of AI, and different meta-heuristics has been proposed to guide the search process that involves the exploration of large state spaces [6]. In this sense, AI can be seen as a basic tool for decision-making by searching for the best sequence of actions or configuration to optimize a function. The integration of DS with meta-heuristic can help afford the complexity of scheduling activities, planning a production, or managing resources for complex systems such as those emerging in Cyber-physical systems, Industry 4.0, Digital Twins and Smart environments.

However, the applicability of search-based approaches are often limited by the state-space explosion problem. Of special interest is the integration of DS with meta-heuristic methods that are easily parallelizable [8]. Three modes of DS have been identified to speed-up the exploration of the state-space [11]: 1) To exploit the parallelism of a single simulation; 2) to build and simulate large models by federating simulators, reducing the cost of developing new models; and 3) running simultaneously the same model with different parameters.

The use of DS for single-state methods allow the exploration of large-scale models, and population methods are most readily parallelizable, since they already can simultaneously explore candidate solutions. Even cutting-edge techniques such Deep Reinforcement Learning (DRL), are often limited by its excessive training time dues to the state-space explosion problem [5,7].

On the other direction, regarding the application of AI to DS, it is necessary to design intelligent algorithms that automate the process of looking for the best system configuration. It includes the use of AI to manage the complexity of the simulation task itself in its different phases: model partition and deployment; resource allocation; tuning the distributed simulation in runtime; extraction, storage and compression of the simulation results; and exploitation of the results and traces of the simulation.

The main idea is the use of meta-heuristics such as simulating annealing or genetic algorithms for the definition of the initial partitioning, and DRL for a dynamic model partitioning. It implies a clear definition of the state in each simulation engine and their neighbours, and the actions available to improve the configuration. The work will focus on evaluating metrics for use with the dynamic load balancing mechanism in distributed simulations.

Framework to Support Decision-making based of AI and Simulation of Large-scale Models

Universidad Zaragoza

Unai Arronategui, José Ángel Bañares, José Manuel Colom
unai@unizar.es, banares@unizar.es, jm@unizar.es

1. Framework for Simulation of large scale PN models

- **Simbot: micro-Kernel of Simulation**
  - Efficient interpretation of Flat Timed Petri nets
  - Flattening and Elaboration of High Level Petri nets
  - Compiler for generating efficient execution code
- **Model Driven Engineering approach supported by a PN-based formalism**
  - Languages and tools (HLPN modelling, elaboration, compiler)
  - Configuration language of code deployment for distributed simulation

2. Scalable Compilation & Dynamic Configuration

- **Modular Compilation**
  - Modular/Distributed compilation and linking
  - Model deployment on hybrid clouds (mini-clusters, cloud)
- **Load Balancing mechanism**
  - Model partition
  - Dynamic balancing at different levels of parallelisms
  - Event, Component
- **Artificial Intelligence for Dynamic Configuration**
  - Metaheuristics for model partition
  - Deep Reinforcement Learning for dynamic load-balancing

SCALABILITY

3. Artificial Intelligence and Simulation

- **Large Scale Simulations for Exploration & AI training**
  - Optimization problems:
    - Exploration of large scale state spaces
    - Speed up the search
  - Parallelization of Metaheuristics
- Training Agents in Large scale simulated Environments

Population

Agent — Policy Function — Update — Reinforcement Learning
actions — rewards — sensors
Simulated Environment

Large Scale Simulation Framework

Problem Domain | Functional level | Operational Level

Conceptual Modelling
Conceptual Model
Verification Model

Hierarchical PN model
HLPN

Translate to PN
M&S, Analysis & making decisions workflow

Qualitative Analysis — Quantitative Analysis

Qualitative results
- Properties verification
- Structural bounds.
- Properties validation
- Deadlock Freeness

Quantitative Results
- Resource profiling
- Component Simulation on target platform

Elaboration
Platform Profiling
Operational model

Profiling results
Lefs Code

Conceptual model

Flat lef-code PN model

Results Collection
name Server

Optimizing partitions
- Lookahead
- Structural conflicts
- work load metrics

Simbots system

Conceptual Modelling — model refinement
Execution, Monitoring, Load balancing
Analysis & Model Refinement

Model partition and Deployment
Model partition & Deployment
Compilation & Deployment
Code for Distributed Simulation
Distributed Simulation Execution
Profiling, validation

GECON 2022 19th International Conference on the Economics of Grids, Clouds, Systems, and Services – 13-15 September, 2022, Izola, Slovenia

4   Future Work

In our previous work we have developed a PN based framework for M&S of large scale and complex systems. Previous works has described a PN based modular language, the translation of the PN to a representation for efficient distributed simulation, the algorithms for distributed simulation and load-balancing mechanism. Future work will focus in the incorporation of AI in two directions: to adapt meta-heuristics algorithms to take advantage of distributed simulation of large systems; and the incorporation of AI to take decisions on runtime using developed mechanisms to obtain the best configuration.

Acknowledgments. This work was co-financed by the Aragonese Government and the European Regional Development Fund "Construyendo Europa desde Aragón" (COSMOS research group); and by the Spanish program "Programa estatal del Generación de Conocimiento y Fortalecimiento Científico y Tecnológico del Sistema de I+D+i", project PGC2018-099815-B-100.

References

1. Arronategui, U., Bañares, J.Á., Colom, J.M.: A MDE approach for modelling and distributed simulation of health systems. In: Djemame, K., Altmann, J., Bañares, J.Á., Agmon Ben-Yehuda, O., Stankovski, V., Tuffin, B. (eds.) GECON 2020. LNCS, vol. 12441, pp. 89–103. Springer, Cham (2020). https://doi.org/10.1007/978-3-030-63058-4_9
2. Bañares, J.Á., Colom, J.M.: Model and simulation engines for distributed simulation of discrete event systems. In: Coppola, M., Carlini, E., D'Agostino, D., Altmann, J., Bañares, J.Á. (eds.) GECON 2018. LNCS, vol. 11113, pp. 77–91. Springer, Cham (2019). https://doi.org/10.1007/978-3-030-13342-9_7
3. Bartz-Beielstein, T., Filipič, B., Korošec, P., Talbi, E.-G. (eds.): High-Performance Simulation-Based Optimization. SCI, vol. 833. Springer, Cham (2020). https://doi.org/10.1007/978-3-030-18764-4
4. Bergero, F., Kofman, E.: A vectorial devs extension for large scale system modeling and parallel simulation. SIMULATION **90**(5), 522–546 (2014)
5. Capocchi, L., Santucci, J.F.: Discrete event modeling and simulation for reinforcement learning system design. Information **13**(3), 121 (2022)
6. Hussain, K., Salleh, M.N.M., Cheng, S., Shi, Y.: Metaheuristic research: a comprehensive survey. Artif. Intell. Rev. **52**(4), 2191–2233 (2019)
7. Körber, M., Lange, J., Rediske, S., Steinmann, S., Glück, R.: Comparing popular simulation environments in the scope of robotics and reinforcement learning (2021). https://arxiv.org/abs/2103.04616
8. Luke, S.: Essentials of Metaheuristics, 2nd edn. (2013). http://cs.gmu.edu/sean/book/metaheuristics/
9. Meraji, S., Tropper, C.: Optimizing techniques for parallel digital logic simulation. IEEE Trans. Parallel Distrib. Syst. **23**(6), 1135–1146 (2012)
10. Rabe, M., Deininger, M., Juan, A.A.: Speeding up computational times in simheuristics combining genetic algorithms with discrete-event simulation. Simul. Model. Pract. Theory **103**, 102089 (2020)
11. Taylor, S.J.: Distributed simulation: state-of-the-art and potential for operational research. Eur. J. Oper. Res. **273**(1), 1–19 (2019)

A Game-Theoretic Approach for Pricing and Determining Quality Levels of Cybersecurity Products Under an Exogenous Information-Sharing Program

Morteza Rasti-Barzoki[1,2,3], Jörn Altmann[2,3(✉)], and Bernhard Egger[4]

[1] Department of Industrial and Systems Engineering, Isfahan University of Technology, 84156-83111 Isfahan, Iran
rasti@cc.iut.ac.ir
[2] Institute of Engineering Research, College of Engineering, Seoul National University, Seoul 08826, South Korea
jorn.altmann@acm.org
[3] Technology Management Economics and Policy Program, College of Engineering, Seoul National University, Seoul 08826, South Korea
[4] Department of Computer Science and Engineering, College of Engineering, Seoul National University, Seoul 08826, South Korea
bernhard@csap.snu.ac.kr
https://rasti.iut.ac.ir/

Abstract. Price and quality level of products are two important decisions of any business. This paper provides equilibrium solutions for these decisions of two players for a cybersecurity ecosystem, including a solution provider and an information provider. We assume that end users join a cybersecurity ecosystem based on the prices and qualities of the solution provider's and information provider's products; so that, the increasing of the prices or/and decreasing the qualities will reduce the number of end-users of that ecosystem. Also, it is assumed that there is an exogenous information-sharing program under which the effect of quality of the information provider's product on the cybersecurity level depends on the level of information-sharing. Under this information-sharing program, the equilibrium solutions of prices and qualities of these two players are given. Also, some results and insights are given with a numerical example.

Keywords: Cybersecurity Ecosystem · Pricing · Quality Level · information Sharing · Game Theory

1 Introduction

The enterprise information systems security directly affects other firms, and the interconnectedness of information assets inevitably affects the choice of strategy of information security. Also, information-sharing (InSh) is a strategic complementary relationship to information security investments. By InSh between companies, companies can reduce

© The Author(s), under exclusive license to Springer Nature Switzerland AG 2023
J. Á. Bañares et al. (Eds.): GECON 2022, LNCS 13430, pp. 153–157, 2023.
https://doi.org/10.1007/978-3-031-29315-3_15

the security cost and improve the information security level [1]. Therefore, companies can benefit from InSh [2–4]. However, with the expansion of information and communication technology, the InSh efficiency is not fully understood [5]; Therefore, it is very important to develop economic models in which InSh and product quality are considered together. For details of literature refer to [1, 5–10]. To our knowledge, there is no research that has formulated a security ecosystem issue from a supply chain perspective. The under-hand paper tries to find the equilibrium solutions of two important players of a cybersecurity ecosystem including a solution provider and an information provider. Due to the nature of the problem, game theory has been used to find equilibrium solutions. The research questions of this study are as follows. *RQ 1. What are the equilibrium prices and qualities under the InSh program? RQ 2. How do parameters affect player profits? RQ 3. Are there any conditions under which the players' equilibrium profits improve significantly?*

2   Problem Description

Parameters	
υ	A fixed value in the function of number of end-users (the number of end-users when the security level and prices are close to zero)
α	Demand sensitivity to the security level
γ	Demand sensitivity to the price level
c_S	Cost of the solution provider's product
c_I	Cost of the information provider's product
θ_S	Coefficient of the effect of the quality level of the solution provider's product on the solution provider costs
θ_I	Coefficient of the effect of the quality level of the information provider's product on the information provider costs
ψ	Information-sharing level
Decision variables	
p_S	Price of the solution provider's product
p_I	Price of the information provider's product
q_S	Quality level of the solution provider's product
q_I	Quality level of the information provider's product
Demand and profit functions	
U	Number of installed-base or end-users
L	The level of cybersecurity
π_S	Profit function of the solution provider
π_I	Profit function of the information provider

Consider a solution provider and an information provider in a cybersecurity ecosystem, each of which wants to determine the price and quality of its product. For brevity, we refer to [11] for definitions and roles of cybersecurity ecosystem's agents. The number of customers of this ecosystem is a function of the prices and qualities of the solution provider's and information provider's products. Increasing the quality increases the number of customers and increasing the price reduces the number of customers. The profit of these two players is a function of price, cost of each product unit, and costs of increasing product quality. Due to the frequent use of linear functions in the related literature, the linear functions are used to formulate the effect of price and quality on the number of end-users of this ecosystem. Therefore, according to the defined notations and the above explanations, the number of customers of this ecosystem is calculated by Eq. (1). The cybersecurity level and the profit functions of two considered players are provided in Eqs. (2)–(4), respectively. The demand for cybersecurity products increases with the increase in the security level of that product and the decrease in its price. This issue is formulated in Eq. (1). The level of cybersecurity increases by increasing the quality of the solution and information providers (Eq. (2)) but this effect may not be the same in general; so, we added ψ to model different effects. Equations (3)–(4) show the profits, which are equal to revenue minus quality cost. In this research, we look for interior solutions, so all the functions should be considered positive.

$$U = \upsilon + \alpha L - \gamma (p_S + p_I) \tag{1}$$

$$L = q_S + \psi q_I \tag{2}$$

$$\pi_S = (p_S - c_S)U - \theta_S q_S^2 \tag{3}$$

$$\pi_I = (p_I - c_I)U - \theta_I q_I^2 \tag{4}$$

Game theory is widely used in the literature to analyze a wide range of multi-player decision problems. The equilibrium solutions of decision variables of the solution provider and the information provider are provided in **Theorem** 1 based on **Lemma** 1.

Lemma 1. π_S On p_S and q_S and π_I on p_I and q_I are jointly concave functions if $\alpha < 2\sqrt{\gamma \theta_S}$ and $\alpha < \frac{2}{\psi}\sqrt{\gamma \theta_I}$, respectively.

*Theorem 1. The equilibrium solutions of prices and qualities of the two players are provide in Eqs. (5)–(8). The necessary conditions were provided in **Lemma** 1.*

$$p_S^{NE} = c_S + \frac{2\theta_I\theta_S(\upsilon - (c_I + c_S)\gamma)}{6\gamma\theta_I\theta_S - \alpha^2(\theta_I + \theta_S\psi^2)} \qquad (5)$$

$$q_S^{NE} = \frac{\alpha\theta_I(\upsilon - (c_I + c_S)\gamma)}{6\gamma\theta_I\theta_S - \alpha^2(\theta_I + \theta_S\psi^2)} \qquad (6)$$

$$p_I^{NE} = c_I + \frac{2\theta_I\theta_S(\upsilon - (c_I + c_S)\gamma)}{6\gamma\theta_I\theta_S - \alpha^2(\theta_I + \theta_S\psi^2)} \qquad (7)$$

$$q_I^{NE} = \frac{\alpha\theta_S(\upsilon - (c_I + c_S)\gamma)\psi}{6\gamma\theta_I\theta_S - \alpha^2(\theta_I + \theta_S\psi^2)} \qquad (8)$$

Corollary 1. *Equilibrium prices and quality of solution provider and information provider's products have the following relationships with each other (See Eqs. (9) and (10)). Therefore:*

- *According to Eq. (9), the marginal profits of two considered players are the same and is equal to $\frac{2\theta_I\theta_S(\upsilon - (c_I + c_S)\gamma)}{6\gamma\theta_I\theta_S - \alpha^2(\theta_I + \theta_S\psi^2)}$.*
- *According to Eq. (10), for each specific value of the InSh level, the ratio of quality of solution provider's product to quality of information provider's product varies by a factor of θ_S/θ_I. This relationship also shows that with the increasing of the level of InSh or/and increasing the quality cost coefficient of solution provider's product or decreasing the quality cost coefficient of information provider's product, the difference between the qualities of two products increases.*

$$p_S^{NE} - c_S = p_I^{NE} - c_I = \frac{2\theta_I\theta_S(\upsilon - (c_I + c_S)\gamma)}{6\gamma\theta_I\theta_S - \alpha^2(\theta_I + \theta_S\psi^2)} \qquad (9)$$

$$\frac{q_I^{NE}}{q_S^{NE}} = \frac{\theta_S}{\theta_I}\psi \qquad (10)$$

3 Summary

This article presents the equilibrium solutions of two players in cybersecurity enhancement, including the solution provider and the information provider. Equilibrium solutions of prices and qualities of products are provided for these two players. This article can be expanded to consider other aspects of cybersecurity, such as corporate awareness and the role of government in improving security.

Acknowledgements. This work was supported by the Korean Ministry of Science and ICT through the National Research Foundation (NRF) of Korea Grant No. NRF-2021H1D3A2A01082266 (Brain Pool program) and by NRF grants 0536–20210093 and 21A20151113068 (BK21 Plus for Pioneers in Innovative Computing - Dept. of Computer Science and Engineering, SNU). The Institute of Engineering Research (IOER) and the Institute of Computer Technology (ICT) at Seoul National University provided research facilities for this study.

References

1. Li, X., Xue, Q.: An economic analysis of information security investment decision making for substitutable enterprises. Manage. Decis. Econ. **42**(5), 1306–1316 (2021)
2. Cui, R., et al.: Information sharing in supply chains: an empirical and theoretical valuation. Manage. Sci. **61**(11), 2803–2824 (2015)
3. Scott, E.D.: Police Information Sharing: All-Crimes Approach to Homeland Security. LFB Scholarly Pub (2009)
4. Brilingaitė, A., et al.: Overcoming information-sharing challenges in cyber defence exercises. J. Cybersecur. **8**(1), tyacc001 2022
5. Xin, Y., Ran, C., Liu, D.: Incentive and game of information sharing based on blockchain technology. J. Phys: Conf. Ser. **2173**(1), 012034 (2022)
6. Kianpour, M., Kowalski, S.J., Øverby, H.: Systematically understanding cybersecurity economics: a survey. Sustainability **13**(24), 13677 (2021)
7. Li, X.: Decision making of optimal investment in information security for complementary enterprises based on game theory. Technol. Anal. Strateg. Manage. **33**(7), 755–769 (2021)
8. Collins, B., Xu, S., Brown, P.N.: Paying firms to share cyber threat intelligence. In: Bošanský, B., Gonzalez, C., Rass, S., Sinha, A. (eds.) GameSec 2021. LNCS, vol. 13061, pp. 365–377. Springer, Cham (2021). https://doi.org/10.1007/978-3-030-90370-1_20
9. Li, X.: An evolutionary game-theoretic analysis of enterprise information security investment based on information sharing platform. Manag. Decis. Econ. **43**, 595–606 (2021)
10. Grigoryan, G., Collins, A.J.: Game theory for systems engineering: a survey. Int. J. Syst. Syst. Eng. **11**(2), 121–158 (2021)
11. Rashid, Z., Noor, U., Altmann, J.: Economic model for evaluating the value creation through information sharing within the cybersecurity information sharing ecosystem. Futur. Gener. Comput. Syst. **124**, 436–466 (2021)

Design and Implementation of a Compiler for Simulation of Large-Scale Models

Tomás Pelayo, Unai Arronategui⬛, José Ángel Bañares⁽⊠⁾⬛,
and José Manuel Colom⬛

Aragón Institute of Engineering Research (I3A), University of Zaragoza,
Zaragoza, Spain
{779691,unai,banares,jm}@unizar.es

Abstract. As systems become increasingly sophisticated, their state
spaces become larger and the use of analysis and simulation techniques is
impossible by a single-processor machine. Distributed simulation seems
the natural way to afford this problem. However, the main bottleneck of
distributed simulation is the management, compilation and deployment
of large scale models. This paper presents the experimentation results of
a compiler of large scale Petri-net based models.

Keywords: Distributed simulation · Timed Petri nets · Large-scale
compilation

1 Introduction

As systems become complex their modelling involves the management of large
scale models, and their analysis and simulation becomes infeasible. Modular
design and distributed simulation (DS) are the silver-bullets to manage large-
scale modelling ans simulation. However the complexity of distributed simulation maintains recurrent challenges. The pessimism has spread among the M&S
community due to the difficulties to bring the field to a commercial success for
performance prediction of complex, scalable systems [2].

The cloud has proven to be a suitable platform for distributed simulation
of discrete event systems [5]. However, the incorporation of economic cost and
energy consumption, in addition to the traditional speed-up metric have made
DS even more complicated, especially if we are considering large-scale models.

Petri nets (PN) are a well-known formalism for M&S of complex systems such
as the cloud [4]. PN formal verification methods and simulation allow quantitative and qualitative analysis. Our previous works has defined a PN-based framework for the M&S of large scale models that provides a conceptual modelling
language, a representation code for efficient distributed interpretation, mechanisms for load-balancing, and the overall methodology [1]. This paper focuses on
the main bottleneck to develop large-scale models: A compiler and distributed
linker to translate large scale models to executable models on a distributed execution platform.

J. Á. Bañares et al. (Eds.): GECON 2022, LNCS 13430, pp. 158–162, 2023.
https://doi.org/10.1007/978-3-031-29315-3_16

The remainder of this paper is organised as follows: The first section briefly presents the incorporation of modular and hierarchical structuring primitives for defining large scale models. Section 3 briefly describes the design and implementation details of a compiler and distributed linker, and presents some preliminary experimental results. Finally, in Sect. 4 we provide some final remarks.

2   Modular Design of Complex and Large Scale TPN Models

Complex Systems are composed by a large number of entities whose behaviour and interactions (communications, competing for resources, etc.) can be modelled by Timed Petri nets (TPN). To build large scale distributed simulations it is necessary to decompose the conceptual model into components, each of which can be separately compiled to generate executable code for simulation. The composition of TPN-based specifications can be done by the incorporation of structuring mechanism (components) and mechanism for TPN composition [3] based on place/transition fusion, or arc connections. The interface of components includes input and output port specifications, and primitives for composing component behaviours by means of port connections.

A basic component can have in, out and inout ports. They specify sending and receiving events between components, and they are translated internally to places, transitions, and arcs. The mapping of in and out ports translates into a fusion of places, and inout port mappings represents a rendez-vous that can be translated into a fusion of transitions. Figure 1a represents a graphical representation of a basic component. A composite represents an aggregation of components, the port mapping between them, and what subcomponent ports configure the composite interface. Figure 1b shows the graphical representation of a composite.

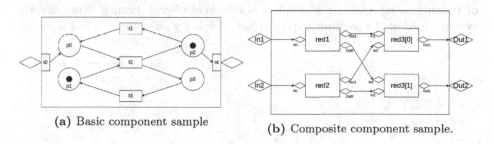

(a) Basic component sample

(b) Composite component sample.

Fig. 1.

3   Model Elaboration, Compilation, and Distributed Linked

Code execution for the simulation is based on the PN interpretation, which allow to separate the model specification from the simulator. It is essential for scaling simulations and simplifying the dynamic deployment of simulation code on distributed execution platforms. To provide an efficient interpretation, the specification must be translated to a model representation that allow the efficient interpretation of the model (fast update of the list of enabled transition).

In previous works [1], we presented a TPN representation suitable for efficient distributed simulation based on linear enabling functions (LEFs). In a first step, the compiler translates the hierarchical description of components are flattened by a called *elaboration* process that produces a flat TPN representation. Then, The compiler translates the intermediate PN representation to an event dependency network, where each transition is translated to a structure that represents the transition enabling state, and how to update the enabling state of those transitions affected by the occurrence/firing of this transition.

Last step is the translation of code for a centralized simulation, that is, all the computational load of the simulation falls on a single machine, or simulation in a distributed simulator using several nodes. In the case of a distributed simulation, components specified in the top level of the hierarchy is used as the initial model partition to be deployed in the execution platform. To establish the communication channels, we have opted for the composition of components by fusion of transitions. In this way, the linking process recovers the lef structures of connected transitions, it generates the lef structure of the fusion transitions, and replaces fusion transitions by the transition that represents the *rendezvous* that is placed in any of the connected components.

The use of array, iterators and distributed link has an important impact in the required memory to generate the code. Vectors allow load the component only once in memory and use it as a reference for the different vector instances (modules). Replicated modules are connected by the distributed linker.

Our experimental evaluation is based on a synthetic PN that can be easily parametrised with the number of branches, which are chains of events that can be executed in parallel without violating the causality constraint, and the number of transitions represents the simulation workload of each branch. Branches are synchronized at the beginning and the end. This is a good sample to test compiler

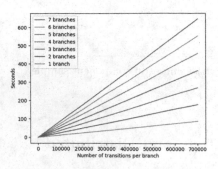

(a) Compilation time with branches.

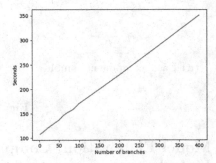

(b) Compilation & link time in function of #branches.

Fig. 2.

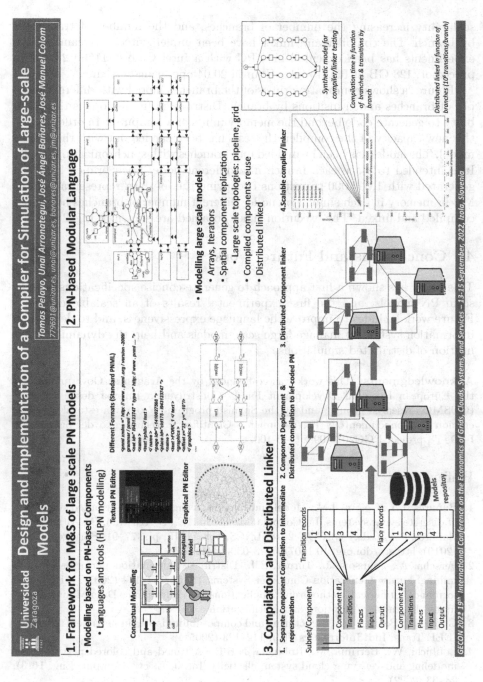

Design and Implementation of a Compiler for Simulation of Large-scale Models

Universidad Zaragoza

Tomas Pelayo, Unai Arronategui, José Angel Bañares, José Manuel Colom
779691@unizar.es, unai@unizar.es, banores@unizar.es, jm@unizar.es

1. Framework for M&S of large scale PN models

- **Modelling based on PN-based Components**
  - Languages and tools (HLPN modelling)

Conceptual Modelling

Textual PN Editor

Graphical PN Editor

2. PN-based Modular Language

Different Formats (Standard PNML)

Modelling large scale models
- Arrays, Iterators
- Spatial component replication
- Large scale topologies: pipeline, grid
- Compiled components reuse
- Distributed linked

Synthetic model for compiler/linker testing

4.Scalable compiler/linker

Compilation time in function of branches & transitions by branch

Distributed linked in function of branches (10⁶ transitions/branch)

3. Compilation and Distributed Linker

1. Separate Component Compilation to Intermediate representation
2. Component Deployment & Distributed compilation to lef-coded PN
3. Distributed Component linker

Models repository

Subnet/Component

Transition records

Place records

Component #1
- Transitions
- Places
- Input
- Output

Component #2
- Transitions
- Places
- Input
- Output

scalability increasing the number of branches, and the number of transitions by branch. The compiler and linker have been implemented in Ocaml. These experiments has been executed in a PC with a Intel Core i7-11700 2.50 GHz processor, 128 GB of RAM and a Ubuntu 20.04 operating system.

Figure 2a shows compilation times of the branches model with different number of branches and transitions by branch. Distributed linking opens the possibility to generate code beyond the memory limits of a computer. In order to test this new capacity of the compiler, the tests has been carried out with the branch model. The model has been be divided into branches with synchronization points. It is intended to place each branch in a different node. Each branch has been generated with 1,000,000 transitions occupying the lef data representation 210 MB in memory in each simulation node. Different number of branches have been compiled and linked. The execution times obtained are shown in Fig. 2b.

4   Conclusions and Future Work

This paper has shown a first approach to generate concise specifications of large scale PN models, and the first experimental results of an scalable compiler. Future work includes to improve the language expressiveness, and to develop an information system to manage large scale models and help the dynamic configuration of distributed simulations.

Acknowledgments. This work was co-financed by the Aragonese Government and the European Regional Development Fund "Construyendo Europa desde Aragón" (COSMOS research group); and by the Spanish program "Programa estatal del Generación de Conocimiento y Fortalecimiento Científico y Tecnológico del Sistema de I+D+i", project PGC2018-099815-B-100.

References

1. Bañares, J.Á., Colom, J.M.: Model and simulation engines for distributed simulation of discrete event systems. In: Coppola, M., Carlini, E., D'Agostino, D., Altmann, J., Bañares, J.Á. (eds.) GECON 2018. LNCS, vol. 11113, pp. 77–91. Springer, Cham (2019). https://doi.org/10.1007/978-3-030-13342-9_7
2. Ferscha, A., Johnson, J., Turner, S.J.: Distributed simulation performance data mining. Future Generation Computer Systems **18**(1), 157–174 (2001). i. High Performance Numerical Methods and Applications. II. Performance Data Mining: Automated Diagnosis, Adaption, and Optimization
3. Gomes, L., Barros, J.P.: Structuring and composability issues in petri nets modeling. IEEE Trans. Ind. Informatics **1**(2), 112–123 (2005)
4. Louhichi, W., Berrima, M., Robbana, N.B.R.: A timed and colored petri nets for modeling and verifying cloud system elasticity. Int. J. Electr. Comput. Eng. **16**(3), 24–33 (2022)
5. Vanmechelen, K., De Munck, S., Broeckhove, J.: Conservative distributed discrete-event simulation on the amazon EC2 cloud: an evaluation of time synchronization protocol performance and cost efficiency. Simul. Model. Pract. Theory **34**, 126–143 (2013)

Author Index

J. Á. Bañares et al. (Eds.): GECON 2022, LNCS 13430, p. 163, 2023.
https://doi.org/10.1007/978-3-031-29315-3

Printed in the United States
by Baker & Taylor Publisher Services